The Mayfield Quick View Guide
to the Internet

for Intimate Relationships, Sexuality, and Marriage and the Family

M. Paz Galupo
Towson University

Jennifer Campbell
University of Tennessee, Knoxville

Michael Keene
University of Tennessee, Knoxville

Mayfield Publishing Company
Mountain View, California
London • Toronto

International Standard Book Number 0-7674-0730-X

Manufactured in the United States of America
10 9 8 7 6 5 4 3 2 1

 This book is printed on recycled paper.

Mayfield Publishing Company
1280 Villa Street
Mountain View, California 94041

The Internet addresses listed in the text were accurate at the time of publication. The inclusion of a Web site does not indicate an endorsement by the authors or Mayfield Publishing Company, and Mayfield does not guarantee the accuracy of the information presented at these sites.

CONTENTS

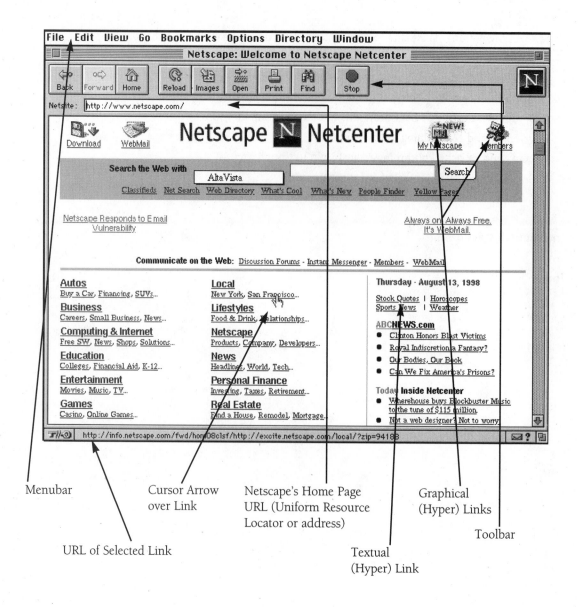

Menubar

Cursor Arrow
over Link

Netscape's Home Page
URL (Uniform Resource
Locator or address)

Graphical
(Hyper) Links

Toolbar

URL of Selected Link

Textual
(Hyper) Link

INTRODUCTION

What Can the Internet Do for You?

The Internet is a vast resource not only for information, entertainment, and interaction with other people in other places who share your interests, but also for learning. You can do everything from reading newspapers and magazines to learning how to create your own Web page, to videoconferencing, to watching video clips from your favorite movies, to downloading free software for your computer, to taking a virtual tour of Hawaii or a human heart. The Internet often has the most current news, the best views of weather anywhere, the best maps, and up-to-the-minute discussions of current events. Additionally, it is convenient to have a variety of dictionaries, thesauruses, and encyclopedias on hand while writing a paper.

Beyond all those uses, *the Internet frees you from the physical boundaries of your hometown, your campus, your city, your state, and your country.* Information from Japan or Germany or Australia can come to you just as fast and easily as information from across the hall. Because the Internet does not have opening or closing hours, its information is more accessible than the information in your library. It does not matter if your school's library is tiny; with access to the Internet, you have more information at your fingertips than the biggest library anywhere. All you need to do is learn how to find it. To help you find information on the Internet quickly and document it correctly is the purpose of this book.

What Are the Internet and the World Wide Web?

The Internet is a global network of computers. It is composed of many parts, such as Web documents, e-mail, Telnet, file transfer, Usenet (newsgroups), and Gopher. The Internet was user hostile until the **World Wide Web** came along. *The Web is a huge number of sites of information within the Internet.* Not only does the Web make accessing the Internet easier, but it also makes the Internet more fun because of the Web's **hypermedia** capabilities, such as audio, video, 3-D images, virtual reality, real-time communication, and animation. So let us help you get started!

QUICK VIEW
HOW CAN I USE GRAPHICAL ACCESS TO THE INTERNET?

Some students have access to computers that already have Netscape, Explorer, or some other graphical browser. If that's your situation, this page will get you off to a fast start. The rest of this guide will provide more detailed directions.

Using Netscape and Other Graphical Browsers

To access the Web's multimedia capabilities, you need a graphical **browser,** such as Netscape's Navigator or Microsoft's Internet Explorer. (Note: You also need **TCP/IP** software; see page 4.) Netscape is used in the following description; other browsers, such as Explorer, work in essentially the same way.

Click on the Netscape icon to launch the program. The first Web page you see will depend on your **Internet service provider (ISP).** Most providers have designated a Web page to appear when you start Netscape. Many people like their first screen to be a search engine, such as Yahoo! <http://www.yahoo. com>. The Netscape Help button will show you how to change your start-up page.

There are several ways to access a **Web page** using Netscape. First, you can follow a **hyperlink,** which can be either text or an image. Textual hyperlinks, or **hypertext,** have a different look from the rest of the text. Depending on the browser you use, hypertext will either be a different color or it will be underlined, or both. To follow a **link,** use your mouse to drag the arrow over the hypertext. When positioned over a link, the arrow will turn into a hand. Click the mouse, and you will go to that Web page. (Some links on some pages are not marked, but whenever your cursor arrow turns into a hand, you can click there and be taken somewhere else.)

Another option to clicking a link is to type out a page's address (called the **uniform resource locator,** or **URL**). Click on the Open button on the toolbar, type the URL in the box provided, and press Return. To navigate through a sequence of pages you have already seen, use the Back and Forward buttons on the toolbar. You may also access a Web page you have already seen by choosing it from your list of **Bookmarks,** from entries on the History list (from the Window menu), or from the Go menu.

(Note: Most URLs in this book are enclosed in angle brackets, < >, for readability. They are not part of the address.)

QUICK VIEW
How Can I Use Text-Only Access to the Internet?

Some students have access to computers that will give them only text from the Internet. If your computer gives you access to Lynx or some other text-only browser, this page will help you get off to a fast start. The rest of this guide provides more detailed instructions.

Using Lynx and Other Text-Only Browsers

Lynx is the most popular text-only browser. With text-only browsers, you cannot view the multimedia functions on the Web, such as pictures, audio, or video. You see only text. (Note: You do not need TCP/IP software to use Lynx.)

If you have a computer account at school, find out if it is a **UNIX** or VMS account. Chances are it will be a UNIX account. (Lynx runs on both, but our example shows how it works on UNIX.) Next, find out whether Lynx is available; if so, you can access Lynx by logging on to your computer account and then on to Lynx. After logging on, you will see either a $ or a %. Then type lynx. Your screen will look like this:

```
$ lynx
```

The first screen displayed should be a page containing information about the World Wide Web and giving you access to other pages.

To access a specific Web page, type lynx followed by the specific Web page's Internet address (its uniform resource locator, or URL). For example, if you wanted to go to Netscape's **home page,** your command line would look like this:

```
$ lynx http://www.home.netscape.com
```

When you view a Web page, the hypertext links (shortcuts to other pages) will appear in bold. To move your cursor to a link (in bold text), use your up and down arrow keys. When you place your cursor on the bold text, the text will become highlighted. To follow the link, press the right-arrow key. To go back, press the left-arrow key.

At the bottom of the screen, you will find a list of other commands. Simply type the first letter in the command name to execute that command. When you are finished, type q to quit. You will be asked if you really want to quit; type y for yes. This will bring you back to your system prompt (the $ or the %).

(Note: Most URLs in this book are enclosed in angle brackets, < >, for readability. They are not part of the address.)

PART ONE
FINDING INFORMATION ON THE INTERNET

The Internet started in the 1960s as a project by the U.S. government to link supercomputers; eventually, its networking technology was used by academic institutions. In the beginning, the Internet was user hostile, and the numbers of computers and people it connected were limited. With the creation of the World Wide Web in the early 1990s by Tim Berners-Lee in Switzerland, the Internet became much more user friendly. Today, the Internet, a global network of computers, has a great many parts: the World Wide Web, Usenet, Gopher, Telnet, and FTP (file transfer protocol).

Technically, the World Wide Web is an Internet facility that uses hypertext to link multimedia sources. Web **servers** store files that can be viewed or downloaded with a Web browser via **HTTP** (hypertext transfer protocol). The most popular text-only browser is Lynx; some popular graphical browsers are Netscape, Explorer, and AOL (America Online).

How the Internet Works—In Brief

To find the information you want, you should know a little about how your computer works with the Internet. That is the subject of the next five sections. If you are not interested in learning more about how computers work, you can skip to the section "How to Find the Information You Want" on page 6.

Hardware and Software

To gain access to the Internet, you need a computer with the appropriate hardware and software and an Internet service provider (ISP). Some popular ISPs are AOL, CompuServe, and Netcom. To access the Internet from home, you need a computer with a **modem** to connect your computer to the phone lines. Most modems run at 28.8K **bps** (bits per second). Faster modems can save you money if you are charged by the amount of time you spend on the Web. You will need a computer that has at least 8 megabytes (MB) of **RAM** (random-access memory). A **byte** is equal to 8 bits. (Note: You will also need to find out the networking capabilities of your ISP; information is transferred only as fast as your ISP's slowest connection.)

For software, you will need TCP/IP (transmission control protocol/Internet protocol, or languages that allow computers to communicate with each other) to provide an interface between your computer and the Internet. If you have a Macintosh, you need MacTCP. If you have an IBM or clone, you need Winsock (which stands for "Windows socket"). Generally these networking protocols are already provided with your computer operating system. There are two main types of browsers: graphical and text-only, explained in more detail on pages 2 and 3.

Client/Server Systems

The Web works on a client/server system. The **client** is your computer and software; a server is any computer that houses files (text, audio, video, software) you want; and **networks** are systems that connect clients and servers. Think of your computer (the client) as a customer in a restaurant and the information provider (the server) as the chef. You order a meal (the information), and the waiter or waitress (the network) brings it back to you (your computer).

URLs and How They Work

To access a file by means of a Web browser, you must know its location. A URL (uniform resource locator), the Internet address for a file, is composed as follows:

```
protocol://server and domain name/file path/file
```

For example, suppose a student named Jane Smith at the University of Tennessee, Knoxville, has created a personal Web page for her résumé. The address for that page is as follows:

```
http://funnelweb.utcc.utk.edu/~jSmith/Resume.html
```

Here, `http` is the **protocol**; `funnelweb.utcc.utk.edu` is the server and **domain name**; `~jSmith` is the **file path**; and `Resume.html` is the file. When we type this address in Netscape or Lynx, the browser reads the URL's components to find the specific page. Our computer has to know what kind of protocol, or language, to speak in order to communicate with the server. The first part of the URL not only tells us what type of file we are accessing, but it also tells the computer what kind of language it needs to speak. In this case, we want a Web page in **HTML** (hypertext mark-up language), so the computer needs to speak hypertext, using HTTP (hypertext transfer protocol).

The next thing our computer needs to know is where the file is kept. This is what the second part of the URL, the server and domain name, tells us. The server where the Web page in this example is kept is called `funnelweb`. The funnelweb server is a computer at the University of Tennessee, Knoxville (UTK) that is denoted by `utcc.utk.edu`. The `.edu` lets us know that the domain is "educational." Other types of domains are `.com` for "commercial," `.mil` for "military," `.org` for "organizational," `.net` for "network," and `.gov` for "governmental" sites. Recently, seven new domain categories were added: `.firm` for "business," `.store` for "retail," `.nom` for "individual," `.rec` for "recreational," `.info` for "informational," `.arts` for "cultural," and `.web` for "Web oriented" sites.

Of all the Web pages at UTK, how does your computer know which one is Jane Smith's? The last two parts of the URL tell how to get to Jane Smith's file. (Note the tilde symbol [~], which lets us know that we are looking for a personal page. This is not unique to UTK, but standard for many personal pages.) The user identification for Jane's file path, or "user area," is `~jSmith`. The file we want is `Resume.html`. Now that our computer knows where to go, which file to get, and how to read it, the computer can display Jane Smith's page in Netscape. Notice that the file name has a mix of upper- and lowercase letters. Most URLs are case sensitive, so be sure to enter the URL exactly, including the uppercase letters. Note also that URLs never contain spaces.

Downloading Information

When you access a page, it sometimes takes a long time for the page to appear on your screen. If you are using Netscape and look at the bottom of the browser window while waiting for a Web page to appear, you should see a percentage of the amount of data transferred. When you access a Web page, a copy of the file is transferred to your computer's memory. This is called **downloading** a file. So, when you are **surfing** the Web, copies of all those Web pages are downloaded to your computer. However, the file is not downloaded all at once; it is transferred in pieces, or **packets**. Depending on the size of the files you are downloading, the length of time it takes for the Web page to appear will vary: A large Web page or a Web page with lots of graphics will slow the transfer. Image files are larger than text files and take longer to download. To shorten the download time in Netscape, turn off Auto Load Images (from the Options menu). To remove the check mark, click on Auto Load Images. To turn Auto Load Images back on, simply click on that line and it will be reactivated. By turning off Images, Web pages containing graphics will download faster, but you will not see any of the graphics automatically. To see the graphics individually, you have to click on the picture frame, or to see all the graphics at once, turn Auto Load Images back on and click on Reload (from the View menu) or on the Reload button on the toolbar.

Internet Service Providers (ISPs)

Before looking into commercial ISPs, check with your college or university's computing center because some schools offer Internet services for home access to students, faculty, and staff. Internet services through your school will probably be the best deal. Although they may not always have the latest upgrades of hardware or software, the price will probably be hard to beat.

If you decide to go with a commercial ISP, you should do some comparison shopping. Think about what you will be using your Internet connection for, such as e-mail, Internet mail, graphical access to the Web, file transfer, Telnet, or storing Web pages. Once you decide what you will need, find out which ISPs offer all those services. After you have gathered a list of possible providers, ask some questions:

- What is the level of customer support, such as online help, user manuals, and telephone support (preferably 24 hours)?
- Is there an installation fee?
- Is there an extra cost for e-mail? If so, is the charge by message, by time, or by size of the message? Is there a storage fee for mail?
- Are there different rates for access at different times of the day?
- Is there a local dial-in number? Will long-distance fees be charged?
- What is the **bandwidth** (size of the bandwidth can affect access speed)?
- Is all the necessary software provided, such as TCP/IP and a browser (such as Netscape or Explorer)?
- Is storage space available for Web pages? If so, what is the charge?
- Are back-up servers available to help maintain continuous access?
- What kind of security is offered?

How to Find the Information You Want

The Internet is a vast and rapidly changing conglomeration of information. Finding your way to the particular piece of information you need can be difficult if you are not familiar with the search options available.

World Wide Web Search Engines

You can search the Web with **search engines** such as Yahoo! or AltaVista; you can search FTP archives with **Archie** and **ArchiePlex**; you can burrow through **Gopher** with **Veronica**, Archie, **Jughead,** and Gopher Jewels; and you can access library computers directly with Hytelnet <http://www.cam.ac.uk/ Hytelnet/>. Sometimes the problem is *not finding enough information;* more often the problem is *finding too much information;* and always the problem is *finding the right information.* Here are some suggestions for solving these problems.

Search engines are computer programs that allow you to find the information you want through key word searches. The search engine provides a text box, into which you type key words associated with the information you want. Most search engines also offer more complex searches involving some variation of **Boolean logic** with the aid of "logical operators," such as AND, OR, and NOT. (Some search engines use a variation of Boolean searching by letting "+" stand for AND and "−" stand for NOT.) Some even offer more advanced searching, such as limiting your search to specific dates or ranking key words in order of appearance within the document.

There are hundreds of search engines for the Internet—too many to discuss here. Two popular and different types of search engines, Yahoo! (a searchable, browsable directory) and AltaVista (a powerful search engine), are briefly described below. For a more extensive list of search engines, see Netscape's list at <http://home.netscape.com/home/internet-search.html>.

Yahoo! <http://www.yahoo.com>. Yahoo! is both a search engine and a directory made of subject trees. A **subject tree** is a hierarchical index system for finding information. You begin with a general subject, such as Medicine, and follow the subject tree's branches to a specific document. Yahoo!'s subject trees begin on its main page, which can be found at its URL.

Yahoo! is a good way to start searching because it looks at only a few key elements. Consequently, Yahoo! is the place to go for general discussions of your topic. To learn more about how to do a search on Yahoo!, click on the Options link located by the text box where you type in your key terms.

AltaVista <http://www.altavista.digital.com>. Unlike Yahoo!, AltaVista does a thorough full-text search of documents for the key terms. If you put a fairly general key term into AltaVista, you will most likely receive hundreds or even thousands of links to pages that may only mention your topic in passing. AltaVista is a good place to search for obscure items or for very specific topics.

If you are getting too many hits for a topic on AltaVista, try doing the same search on Yahoo!; this should cut down the number of possible matches. Likewise, if you are searching on Yahoo! and you are not getting enough matches, try AltaVista.

AltaVista offers both a Simple Search and an Advanced Search. The Advanced Search helps you limit your results by specifying date ranges and ranking key terms. To find out more about Simple and Advanced Searches on AltaVista, click the Help button at the top of the first AltaVista page.

Searching via Key Words

Key word searches may require some imagination if you are not getting the results you hoped for. In most cases, your search was either too narrow or too broad. The tips below should help. Also, when you do find information you want, remember to check it for credibility. (See pages 10–12 on how to judge the reliability of Internet information.)

Narrowing a Search. If you are getting too many **hits** (successful key word matches), try narrowing your search by adding more key terms. Sometimes this will help, because most search engines will look for each of the terms independently but display the pages with the most matches first. Usually, you can narrow your search and make sure that all the key terms appear in the document by using AND between the key terms.

⌐ **Info Bit**—Narrow your search by looking for the most current information (or for the most relevant dates) in the AltaVista Advanced Search by entering a starting and ending date for the information.

⌐ **Info Bit**—Some search engines, such as Yahoo!, allow you to search within document titles only. This will narrow your search results and may give you better sources on your topic.

Broadening a Search. If you are not getting enough hits, you need to broaden your search by deleting some of the more specific key terms or substituting synonyms for the key words you already have listed. For example, for a search about how to make a Web page, you might try several search strings, such as "Web page design," "creating a Web page," and "making a Web page." Also, you may want to try a more general category under which your topic falls. For example, if you want information on homosexual identity formation, but you get only one or two hits, you could try searching for "homosexual identity" or just "homosexual."

⌐ **Info Bit**—The Web is a big place with millions of documents, and it is growing by the hour. Because no single search engine can cover the whole Web, each search engine covers different, although overlapping, territory. If your search does not work with the first engine you use, try running it on several different ones.

⌐ **Info Bit**—Some search engines are designed to find specific topics, such as PsychCrawler at <http://www.psychcrawler.com/plweb/> or PsycSite Home at <http://stange.simplenet.com/psycsite/html>.

Finding Phrases. If you want to find documents containing a specific phrase, such as "Green Bay Packers," put the phrase in double quotation marks to lock them together. Otherwise you will get thousands of pages that have only "green" or "bay" or "packers" in them.

Searching via Subject Trees

As described previously in the section on Yahoo!, a subject tree is a hierarchical index of topics that allows you to begin with a broad category and follow the subject tree's branches down to a specific file. Subject trees can be good places to start your search because you can get an idea of the different types of information available on your topic.

One of the first and best subject trees is The Virtual Library <http://www.w3.org/vl> maintained by the W3 Consortium <http://www.W3.org/pub/WWW>. There are different ways to search The Virtual Library. You can start searching the Subject Index on the main page, or you can search the Category Subtree or the Top Ten Most Popular Fields.

⌐⊟ *Info Byte: Some Common Error Messages*

Connection refused by server	Server is busy. The maximum number of simultaneous connections has probably been reached. Try again later.
Document contains no data	First, try clicking the link again. If this doesn't work, there may be a glitch in the network.
Error 400	Your request could not be understood by the server. Your Web browser may be malfunctioning or your Internet connection may be unreliable. Try shutting down and restarting your computer.
Forbidden access (Error 401)	For some reason, the creator or maintainer of a page does not want any "outside" visitors, and he or she has restricted the access to the page.
No DNS entry	Means "No Domain Name System," or that the server does not exist. If you are linking to the page from another, try clicking the link again. If you are entering the URL, make sure you have entered it correctly—with any capital letters and punctuation and without spaces. If the URL is correct, the server may not be working.
No response	There may be too many connections, or the server may be down for some reason. Try again later.
Not found (Error 404)	The file you are looking for is not on this server. It may have been moved or deleted.
Transfer interrupted!	For some reason, the server was not able to transfer all of the data for this page. Try reloading.

Other Protocols: Telnet and Gopher

Web servers communicate through HTTP, but there are other, older information systems, such as Telnet and Gopher, that communicate through other protocols. The URLs for these other Internet systems begin with a different protocol abbreviation, or prompt, such as `ftp://`, `gopher://`, or `telnet://`. Telnet and Gopher are described here; FTP (file transfer protocol) is discussed in Part Two.

Telnet. Some electronic **bulletin boards,** library catalogs, and school computer accounts are not part of the Web. To access these sources, you need to use **Telnet,** a protocol that lets you communicate with computers that use the UNIX operating system. To use Telnet, you need to log on to another computer (a remote host). When you log on, a text-only screen identical to the screen of the remote host will appear. Then you can issue commands from your computer and have them carried out by the remote host.

A Telnet session's first screen usually lists instructions for logging on, accessing the Help page, and logging off. If you get a blank screen, try pressing Enter (or Return). If you get a screen with instructions, *read it carefully,* because when you want to exit a session, you may not remember how. If no instructions are given, try typing ? and pressing Enter to get the Help page. To exit, hold the Command key and type q if you are using a Macintosh, or hold the Control key and type q if you are using a PC.

To use Telnet, you will need Telnet software. If your ISP does not provide the software, you can download it from the Internet for free. For a Macintosh, get NCSA Telnet at <http://www.ncsa.uiuc.edu/SDG/Software/Brochure/Overview/MacTelnet.overview.html>. For a PC, get EWAN Telnet from ZDNet at <http://www5.zdnet.com>. On the screen that appears, click on the Downloads button. Go to the bottom of the screen and type EWAN in the key word box and click on the Start Search button.

Gopher. Gopher is a menu-driven information system started at the University of Minnesota and named after its mascot, a gopher. It is a predecessor of the World Wide Web. However, Gopher menu systems and files can be accessed via the Web. There is a lot of good information on Gopher that is not available elsewhere on the Internet. If you want to search Gopher, a good place to start is with Gopher Jewels at <http://andromeda.tradewave.com/GJ>. Gopher Jewels catalogs many Gopher sites by subject tree. For a more thorough search of Gopher sites, use a search engine, such as Jughead (document title search) or Veronica (full-text search). For a list of Jughead servers, go to <http://www.yahoo.com/Computers_and_Internet/Internet/Gopher/Searching/Jughead>. To learn more about Veronica, see the **Frequently Asked Questions (FAQs)** page at <gopher://gopher.scs.unr.edu/00/veronica/veronica-faq>. To search using Veronica, go to <gopher://gopher.scs.unr.edu/11/veronica>.

How to Judge the Reliability of Internet Information

Students who are accustomed to doing research in libraries face new issues when they start doing research on the Internet. Before a book or journal appears in a university library, it has usually gone through a number of checks to make sure the information in it is reliable. For example, if you find a copy of *Civilization and Its Discontents* in your university library, you can be sure you are getting a generally accepted version of the real thing. But if you find a copy of *Civilization and Its Discontents* on the Internet, you need to give some thought to *where you found it,* whether the person who put it on the Internet is a *reliable authority on the subject* (someone who can be trusted not to enter his or her own personal, political, or scholarly biases into the text), and whether your professor will *accept your judgment* of the reliability of that material.

Arguably, student researchers should always make these decisions, even about materials they find in the university library. However, judging the reliability of sources found on the Internet is crucial because there is no regulating body that monitors the reliability of what is on the Internet. Although there is so much information on the Internet that it can seem like a university library, it is actually more like a huge open-air market. In one corner there might be reliable sources from whom you can obtain valuable information. But over in another corner there might be weirdos, wackos, and eccentrics, from whom anything you obtain is, at best, questionable. The problem is that on the Internet there is no way to tell the difference. Someone who wants to turn *Civilization and Its Discontents* into an anarchist manifesto can post a rewritten version with no indication of its differences from Sigmund Freud's original. There's a saying in Latin: *caveat emptor,* or "let the buyer beware." When it comes to doing your research on the Internet, the saying should be *caveat internauta,* or "let the surfer beware."

Here is a list of points to consider when you are trying to judge the reliability of information you find on the Internet:

- **Who is the author or sponsor of the page?** On the page you are citing, or on a page linked to it, that individual or organization should be identified, that individual's qualifications should be apparent, and other avenues of verification should be open to you. For a good example of a reliable source, see the "Editorial Board" area for the *Psychological Bulletin* at <http://www.apa.org/journals/bul/editorial%20board.html>. A page created by a person or an organization that does not provide this information is not a good source to cite.

- **Are there obvious reasons for bias?** If the page is presented by a tobacco company consortium, you should be suspicious of its reports on the addictiveness of nicotine. Is there any advertising? If the page is sponsored by Acme Track Shoes, you should be suspicious of its claims for Acme track shoes' performance.

- **Is contact information provided?** If the only identification available is something cryptic, such as "Society for Feruginous Retorts," be suspicious of the page's reliability. If the page is sponsored by a reputable person or organization, there should be some other way to verify that reputation, such as an e-mail or postal address. (Note: A tilde [~] in the page's address usually indicates a personal home page and may require more searching for reliability.)

- **Is there a copyright symbol on the page?** If so, who holds the copyright?

- **Is this page a "zombie,"** or one considered "walking dead" because the person who posted it no longer maintains or updates it? Even though the information is "alive" in that it is still accessible, it is "dead" in that it could well be several years old! Many pages have a "last updated" date.

- **What is the purpose of the page?** Why is this information being posted—as information, as a public service, as a news source, as a research tool for academics, as a personal ax to grind, or as a way to gain attention?

- **How well organized is the page?** Is the page easy to navigate? Is it complete?

- **Is the information on the page *primary* or *secondary*?** That is, is it a report of facts, such as a medical researcher's article describing a new drug treatment for HIV infection, thus making it primary information, or is it an Internet newsgroup discussion about the new drug treatment, thus making it secondary information? The papers and reports you write for your college classes need to be based on primary information whenever possible. The further away from the primary sources your own sources are, the less reliable the information is.

- **Can you verify the information** on the Web page in some other way? For example, can you check the page's bibliography (if there is one) against your library's holdings or check the information against a source in the library?

- **If you are worried that the information may lack credibility, try starting with a source you know is reputable.** For example, if you have to do a project on the latest in cancer research, you can begin your search at major cancer research institutes, such as Mayo Clinic in Rochester, Minnesota <http://www.mayo.edu>.

- Finally, remember that **even though a page might not meet your standards as a citable source, it may help you generate good ideas** or point to other usable sources. Also, be sure not to stop your search at the first page you find—shop around and do some comparing so that you can have points of reference.

Ultimately, the problem with reliability of information on the Web is like the whispering game children play. Someone whispers a message to the first child, who whispers it to the second, and so on. By the time it gets to the last child, the message is hopelessly distorted. Web pages can work the same way when people get their information from other people's Web pages: The first person who posts information may make a few small errors; the second unintentionally repeats them and makes one or two more; the third makes a few more; and so on. For information seekers it can be impossible to tell where in the chain the information is coming from, but that makes a difference in the information's reliability. Remember: It never hurts to check against a library reference.

How to Document Information from Electronic Sources

Whenever you are doing research and writing for a classroom assignment, documenting your sources correctly is important. If the information, ideas, or other kinds of materials (such as drawings and graphics) in your paper are from a source, you need to let your readers know by adding appropriate documentation. (And if you quote passages, you need to add quotation marks or make block quotations as well.) The documentation you provide needs to be complete enough that a reader who wants to check your sources will be able to find them. Material from the Internet and other electronic sources, just like print sources, must be properly documented.

Portable versus Online Sources
There are two kinds of electronic sources of information—*unchangeable* and *changeable*—and they need to be documented in slightly different ways.

   Unchangeable (or Portable) Sources. Suppose you go to the library (or access its collections on a remote computer) and look up material on a **CD-ROM** (compact disk with read-only memory), such as

InfoTrac or some other portable database. As an electronic source, the CD-ROM is stable—that is, anyone could look at it today, next month, or next year, and find the same information. It has a date and place of publication (although here "publication" actually means "production") and a version number, which should be shown in your documentation just as they would be for a journal article. Thus, for unchangeable sources there is no need to add extra elements to your documentation.

Changeable (or Online) Sources. For materials you find on the Internet, you need to add some information to your documentation. Usually, it includes the date you accessed the information and its URL. Sometimes, you may be required to include the path you took to get to the page or even a hard copy (a printout) of the page. If information you find on the Internet is crucial to your work, it is always a good idea to print out a hard copy, just in case.

Different Styles for Different Fields
When you write a paper for a psychology course, you will probably use American Psychological Association (APA) style, which is what academics in the social sciences (such as psychology or sociology) generally use. If you are taking an English composition class, your teacher may require you to use the Modern Language Association (MLA) style, which is what literature and language specialists use. When documenting Web and Internet sources, many teachers of first-year students recommend the Alliance for Computers in Writing (ACW) style <http://english.ttu.edu./acw.html>. Professors for higher-level classes or classes in other fields may expect you to use some other style—the Council of Biology Editors (CBE) style is used in the life sciences; the *Chicago Manual of Style* (CMS) is used in business, history, and many hard sciences; or even the Institute of Electrical and Electronic Engineers (IEEE) style <http://www.ieee.org/guides/style/> is used in fields such as computer science. Although there are hundreds of different styles, the right one for you will probably look close to one of the four varieties presented here.

When and What to Document
Here are six simple guidelines to help you decide when and what to document:

1. If you use the exact language of your source, you must use quotation marks and cite the source.
2. Use direct quotations only if there is something unique about your source's language or if your own words will not do the job better.
3. Directly quote only as much as you need—the bare minimum.
4. If you use information that is not common knowledge, you must cite the source. If this information would not be familiar to someone who had not researched the subject, it is not common knowledge and its source must be cited.
5. Cite all kinds of borrowed information, not just words and facts. Sources can also include drawings, photos, artwork, ideas, music—anything you use that is not yours.
6. To work your quoted or otherwise borrowed material into the text more smoothly, introduce it with the name of the source. To introduce your borrowed material, use a tag line—for example, "As Stanley Prusiner, one of the leading authorities on perception, said . . ."

American Psychological Association (APA) Author-Date Style

APA style places the author's name and date of publication within parentheses in the text, linked to a list of references (titled *References*) at the end of the document. Although the focus of this guide is electronic sources, here is a brief overview of APA documentation style. For more information, consult the *Publication Manual of the American Psychological Association*, 4th edition (1994).

Citations in the Text

Citations in the text generally include the author's last name and the year in parentheses. So a citation to something by Bill Jones in 1988 would be (Jones, 1988). The parenthetical citation precedes the sentence's final punctuation. If the author's name has already appeared in the sentence, the year of publication follows it in parentheses. APA requires page numbers only if you are citing a direct quotation or a specific table, figure, or equation. If you need to include page numbers (and some teachers want page numbers for everything), use *p.* or *pp.*

Parenthetical citations for direct quotations in the text appear after the closing quotation marks but before the final punctuation. If the quotation is more than forty words long, it should be indented an inch. If the quotation is set off, the citation appears after the quotation's final punctuation.

Entries in the References *List*

Each entry in the reference list must match a citation. The entries should be alphabetized by the author's last name and, in the case of multiple entries by one author, listed chronologically, beginning with the earliest. The entire list must be double spaced. APA recommends that the first line of each entry be indented one inch (or five to seven spaces) when materials are submitted for publication, but in APA publications, the first line is flush left and subsequent lines are indented. Each entry has four elements: author, date, title, and publication information. A typical entry for a book looks like this:

> Bordens, K. S., & Abbott, B. B. (1998). <u>Research designs and methods:</u> <u>A process approach</u> (4th ed.). Mountain View, CA: Mayfield.

APA Style for Citing Electronic Sources

APA's style for citing electronic sources is still evolving. The basic citation has five elements: author, date, title, document type, and publication information. The information here has been supplemented by the extension of APA made in *The Mayfield Handbook of Technical and Scientific Writing*.

CD-ROMs and Other Portable Databases

If you use information from a CD-ROM or other unchangeable source (such as a magnetic tape or commercially produced disk), you need to name the author, date, and title just as for a print source. In square brackets after the title, identify the electronic medium. At the end of the entry, give the source location and name of the producer. A typical entry looks like this (because there is no author in this example, the publication's name comes first):

> The world factbook 1994 [CD-ROM]. (1994). Washington, DC: Central
>
> Intelligence Agency [Producer and distributor].

You may encounter a CD-ROM version of a document that is also available in hard copy. If so, your citation needs to include information for both (while making it clear that you accessed the CD-ROM version). This note is for an abstract that was read on CD-ROM:

> Morring, F., Jr. (1994, May 16). Russian hardware allows earlier sta-
>
> tion experiments [CD-ROM]. Aviation Week & Space Technology, 140, 57.
>
> Abstract from: InfoTrac General Periodicals Index-A: Abstract 15482317.

Online Sources

For changeable sources, use this format: author's name, date of the most recent revision (if available), title of the source, and identification of the type of document (such as online serial or personal home page). In place of a publisher is the complete URL, underlined. If the URL will not fit on one line, break it after a period or slash. Finally, the entry includes in parentheses the date you visited that page. Here is an example:

> Land, T. (1996, March 31). Web extension to American Psychological
>
> Association style (WEAPAS) [WWW document] (Rev. 1.2.4). URL http://www.
>
> beadsland.com/weapas/ (visited 1997, April 24).

Modern Language Association (MLA) Author-Page Style

MLA style uses parenthetical citations within the text. They lead readers to a list of entries at the end of the document called *Works Cited*. Generally, the material within the parenthetical citation includes the author's name and the page number to which you are referring. Here we summarize briefly the MLA style of documentation, and on the next page we go into more detail about the MLA style for citing electronic sources. If you want more details about MLA documentation style, consult the *MLA Handbook for Writers of Research Papers*, 4th edition (1995). A basic MLA citation in the text will look like this:

```
. . . leads to better research (Morring 57).
```

This citation would lead readers to the following entry at the end of the document:

```
Morring, Frank, Jr. "Russian Hardware Allows Earlier Space Station
     Experiments." Aviation Week and Space Technology 16 (May 1994): 57.
```

Citations in the Text

In MLA style, parenthetical citations go at the end of the sentence in which the source material appears. If the sentence already includes the author's name, then only the page number appears in the parenthetical citation. In the case of more than one work by the same author, a short title is added in the parentheses. The page number is given in the parentheses, without *p.* or *pp.*

Parenthetical citations for direct quotations in the text appear after the closing quotation marks but before the final punctuation. Direct quotations that are more than four lines long should be indented an inch, rather than being enclosed in quotation marks. The parenthetical reference for such quotations follows the quotation's final punctuation.

Entries in the Works Cited *List*

The list of works cited includes only sources mentioned in the text and not all sources consulted. Entries are arranged alphabetically by the author's last name (or by the first significant word in the title if there is no author). The page is double spaced, with the first line of each entry flush left and subsequent lines indented half an inch (or five spaces on a typewriter). The basic pattern of an entry is author's name, title, and publication information (place, name of publisher, date, and page numbers).

MLA Style for Citing Electronic Sources

The MLA style for citing electronic sources is still evolving. Presented here is information from the current *MLA Handbook* (4th edition) as supplemented by *The Mayfield Handbook of Technical and Scientific Writing*.

CD-ROMs and Other Portable Databases

For unchangeable sources, the citation in the *Works Cited* list includes the author, title, and date information just as for print documents. After the title of the database, there is a period, followed by identification of the medium (such as CD-ROM), another period, and the producer's name and date of the product.

> Morring, Frank, Jr. "Russian Hardware Allows Earlier Space Station
> Experiments." <u>Aviation Week and Space Technology</u> 16 (May 1994): 57.
> <u>InfoTrac: General Periodicals Index</u>. CD-ROM. Information Access.
> Aug. 1996.

Online Sources

For changeable sources, use this format: author's name, full title (articles in quotation marks, books underlined) and any larger document of which it is a part, date of publication or most recent revision (if available), the full URL address enclosed in angle brackets (< >), and the date accessed enclosed in parentheses. Here are two examples:

> Shepherdson, Charles. "History and the Real: Foucault with Lacan."
> <u>Postmodern Culture</u> 5.2 (Jan. 1995): <http://jefferson.village.
> virginia.edu/pmc/shepherd.195.html> (15 May 1995).

> Harnack, Andrew, and Gene Kleppinger. "Beyond the MLA Handbook:
> Documenting Electronic Sources on the Internet." <u>Kairos</u> 1.2 (1996):
> <http://english.ttu.edu/kairos/1.2> (10 Oct. 1996).

Ideally, the URL should not be interrupted by a line break; however, if it is too long to fit on one line, break the URL after a period or slash. Do not put a period after the URL. The same form is used for a document retrieved from a file transfer protocol (FTP) archive, except the abbreviation ftp precedes the address, and the URL is not enclosed in angle brackets.

Council of Biology Editors (CBE) Citation-Sequence System

The CBE style manual presents two systems of documentation. The one summarized here uses numbers in the text that refer to a numbered list of references at the end of the document. Because our purpose here is to show how CBE treats electronic sources, we summarize only the citation-sequence system. For full details, refer to *Scientific Style and Format: The CBE Manual for Authors, Editors, and Publishers,* 6th edition (1994).

Citations in the Text

When a source is first used in the text, it is assigned a number that it retains whenever it is used again. The number appears in superscript immediately after the source is referred to, not separated by a space. If more than one source is cited, the numbers are separated by commas without spaces. Here is a typical entry (taken from *The Mayfield Handbook of Technical and Scientific Writing*):

> The oncogene <u>jun</u> has presently become one of the best-known oncogenes because of its ability to act as a transcription factor[1]. One study[2] examined . . .

Entries in the References List

The sequence of entries in the *References* or *Cited References* list is established by the order in which they appear in the text. The whole list is double spaced. The number of the entry is not indented and is followed by a period. Each entry has four basic elements: author, title, publication information, and page numbers. Authors' first and middle names are abbreviated, as are other elements, and the abbreviations are not followed by periods. Here is an example of a journal article entry:

> 1. Lenski RE, May RM. The evolution of virulence in parasites and pathogens: reconciliation between two competing hypotheses. J Theoret Biol 1994; 169:253-65.

Here is a typical entry for a book:

> 13. Mandelbrot BB. The fractal geometry of nature. San Francisco: WH Freeman; 1995. 460 p.

CBE Style for Citing Electronic Sources

The CBE style for citing electronic sources is still evolving. The pattern for online sources recommended here is taken from *The Mayfield Handbook of Technical and Scientific Writing* and is consistent with other CBE formats.

CD-ROMs and Other Portable Databases

For unchangeable sources, the author, date, and title information is provided just as for a print source. In brackets after the title, identify the medium. At the end of the entry, include the name of the database and its location. Here is a typical entry:

```
9. Morring F Jr. Russian hardware allows earlier station experiments [CD-
     ROM]. Aviat Wk Space Technol 1994;140:57. Abstract from: InfoTrac General
     Periodicals Index-A: Abstract 15482317.
```

Online Sources

The *CBE Manual* does not require the full Internet address for changeable sources. Nonetheless, it makes sense to include this additional information. Here is a sample entry with the type of document provided and the URL and date of access added:

```
1. Brooker MIH, Slee AV. New taxa and some new nomenclature in Eucalyptus.
     Muelleria [abstract online] 1996; 9(75-85). Available from WWW;
     <http://155.187.10.12/cpbr/publications/brooker-slee2.html> (Accessed
     1997 Feb 13.)
```

Chicago Manual of Style (CMS) Superscript System

Three documentation systems are presented in *The Chicago Manual of Style*, 14th edition (1993). The one shown here uses superscript numbers, keyed to numbered endnotes or footnotes. It is based on an adaptation of CMS style for college writers: *A Manual for Writers of Term Papers, Theses, and Dissertations*, 6th edition, by Kate Turabian (1996).

Citations in the Text

Note numbers that appear in the text are superscript numbers. They normally go at the end of the sentence, following the final punctuation; if they must be used within a sentence, they should go after a punctuation mark. CMS superscript notations in the text will look like this:

> One literary critic notes "Austen's uncertainty about the inner life of Darcy,"[1] and another explains that Austen's novels, like those of many other nineteenth-century British authors, empower their heroines "over their own plot" and place them at the center of the action.[2]

If you use a direct quotation in the text, the note number appears after the closing quotation marks. A direct quotation that is eight lines or more should be set off, single spaced, and indented four spaces. The note number appears right after the quotation's final punctuation.

Entries in the Notes List

Each entry in the list of notes should correspond to a superscript number in the text. The entries are arranged numerically, with the reference number followed by a period and a space. The entire list of notes should be double spaced, with the first line of each entry indented half an inch.

Each entry generally has four elements: author, title, publication information, and page numbers. The author's name is given in normal order (first name, then last name). Here is a basic entry for a book:

> 2. Paul C. Cozby, <u>Methods in Behavioral Research,</u> 6th ed. (Mountain View, CA: Mayfield Publishing, 1997), 73.

If note number 3 were to that same source, just a different page, the entry would read

> 3. Ibid., 80.

CMS Style for Citing Electronic Sources

The CMS style for citing electronic sources is still evolving. The pattern for unchangeable sources presented here comes from the current (14th) edition. The pattern for changeable sources comes from the adaptation of CMS style by Kate Turabian (cited on the previous page). An excellent online source for more information about adapting CMS style for online documents is Maurice Crouse's paper "Citing Electronic Information in History Papers," available at <http://www.people.memphis.edu/~mcrouse/elcite.html>.

CD-ROMs and Other Portable Databases

For unchangeable electronic sources, the citation is like that for print sources, with the addition of the name of the producer or vendor and any access numbers associated with the document. Here is a sample entry:

```
    1. Frank Morring, Jr., "Russian Hardware Allows Earlier Station
Experiments," Aviation Week & Space Technology, 16 May 1994, 57; Abstract
15482317: InfoTrac General Periodicals Index-A [CD-ROM],September 1996.
```

Online Sources

For changeable sources, the entry contains the usual elements for print sources, followed by an indication in square brackets of what type of document it is, the complete document address, and the date of access.

```
    2. Charles Shepherdson, "History and the Real: Foucault with Lacan,"
Postmodern Culture 5, no. 2 (January 1995) [serial online]; available from
http://jefferson.village.virginia.edu/pmc/shepherd.195.html; Internet;
accessed 15 May 1995.
```

PART TWO
COMMUNICATING ON THE INTERNET

Part One of this guide explained some of the most important ways people use the Internet to find information. The subject of this part is how to use the Internet to communicate with other people. Of course, making a distinction between these two activities is misleading. For example, when you join an e-mail listserv on the subject of technical communication <listserv@listserv.okstate.edu> because you want to learn more about the field and maybe find an internship, your primary motive may be communication, but you are certainly also finding information.

Communicating on the Internet takes many forms. Here is an overview of the topics discussed in this section:

- E-mail—How to send e-mail to your friends all over the world, how to read e-mail addresses, and how to use Internet mail.
- Netiquette—What you should and shouldn't do when you are communicating on the Internet.
- Discussion groups—How to subscribe to listserv mailing lists (and how to unsubscribe); how to take part in Usenet newsgroups.
- Real-time communication—What is Internet Relay Chat (IRC); what are MOOs, MUDs, MUSHes, and WOOs; what is videoconferencing?
- Electronic file transfer—An introduction to file transfer protocol (FTP) and how to do it.
- Risks and precautions—Find out what you need to know about computer security, disclosing personal information, copyright, libel, plagiarism, and viruses.

How to Communicate with E-Mail

E-mail is a way of sending messages electronically. If you get e-mail service through an ISP, you will be given a mailbox and software for reading and storing your mail, for composing and sending messages, and for creating mailing lists. There are lots of different e-mail software packages available, but they all work in much the same way. Most Web browsers such as Netscape and Explorer have built-in e-mail software.

When someone sends you a message, it will be temporarily stored on your ISP's mail server. You will use your e-mail software to see if you have any messages waiting. If you do, the e-mail software will download them from the mail server to your computer, where you can read, store, delete, reply to, print, or forward them.

When you get an e-mail account, you will be given an e-mail address. The address has three parts: for example, user_name@domain_name. Usually, you will be able to create your own user name, which is how your mailbox is identified. The *at* sign (@) separates the user name from the domain name. The domain name is the name of the computer or system where your e-mail is stored.

In the above e-mail address "user_name" and "domain_name" have no spaces (which is indicated by the underscore)—e-mail addresses cannot have any spaces. The address is also in all lowercase, because e-mail addresses are not case sensitive and are easier to read and type without caps. If you get mail returned because the address could not be found, make sure you have entered it correctly. If you have, and the mail is still returned, the person may have changed addresses or may be having problems with the mail system.

Internet Mail

Internet mail (e-mail sent over the Internet) takes e-mail a step further. For example, suppose you are surfing the Web and find a page that has great information, and you want to get in touch with the person who created the page. Usually the person who created the page will include a link for sending e-mail. When you click the link, a window will appear where you can type and send a message. However, you need **SMTP** (simple mail transfer protocol) to send the message. Check with your ISP for the name of its SMTP server. To receive Internet e-mail, you will also need a **POP** (post office protocol) server. Check with your ISP for a list of services to see if POP mail accounts are available.

Virtual Communities: Listservs and Newsgroups

Virtual communities are ways of organizing or connecting people of like interests over the Internet. In the following section we discuss some modes of communication that are analogous to print newsletters.

Listserv Mailing Lists

Listservs are servers that house **mailing lists.** Listserv mailing lists are discussion groups categorized by special interest. Unlike Usenet newsgroups, which let you browse messages posted on Usenet (discussed next), listserv mail messages are sent directly to your e-mail address. When a member posts a message to the listserv, the message is delivered to every subscriber.

When you subscribe, your name and e-mail address are added to the mailing list. From that point on, you will receive all e-mail messages that are posted to the group. It is always wise to **lurk** (hang out and just read messages) for a while before joining the discussion. When you reply to an e-mail message from a listserv, you can either mail the person who sent the message originally or you can post your response to the entire group.

One way to find a listserv for people with a particular interest is to do a key word search on a search engine, such as Yahoo! or AltaVista, by entering the topic and the word `listserv`. Or you can use search engines that are specifically designed for listservs, such as InterLinks at <http://www.nova.edu/ InterLinks/cgi-bin/lists>. Another good place to search or browse already extensive lists of mailing lists categorized by subject is "Liszt, the Mailing List Directory" at <http://www.liszt.com>.

To subscribe to a list, send an e-mail message to the listserv address. Do not put anything in the subject line of the message. Then, on the first line of the body of the message, type the following:

```
SUB listname [your full name]
```

Once you subscribe, you will receive a set of instructions for list members. It will tell you where to post messages (usually a different address than the subscription address) and what subscription options you have (such as "digest," which combines each day's postings into one packet, or "unsubscribe"). Be sure to save this message!

To unsubscribe, send an e-mail message to the listserv subscription address. Again, do not put

---

⏚ *Info Byte: Netiquette*

As with all human communities, even virtual ones, there is acceptable and unacceptable behavior. **Netiquette,** the guidelines for communicating with others on the Internet, helps us all respect the people who share our cyberspace. Most netiquette guidelines are just common sense, a reminder that even though we're in cyberspace, our relations with others are still human relations. Here are some tips:

- Do not use foul or abusive language.

- Do not force offensive material on unwilling participants.

- Do not join in **flaming** (by sending cruel e-mail to someone). Usually, flaming is started over not-so-common-sense breaches of netiquette.

- Do not shout (that is, do not use all caps) at other people on the Internet.

- Do not take off on tangents that are too far from a discussion group's stated purpose.

- Do not post ambiguous questions or ask questions that are answered in a group's Frequently Asked Questions (FAQs) list.

- Be careful to avoid **spamming,** or sending the same message (like a sales pitch) to many different addresses, especially listservs. Spamming is the equivalent of junk mail and will get you flamed in no time.

- Reread your Internet messages before sending them. Something written in haste may be misread.

---

anything in the subject line of the message. Then, on the first line of the body of the message, type the following:

UNSUB listname [your full name]

Remember to unsubscribe if you terminate your e-mail account. Only you can unsubscribe your name from a list.

Usenet Newsgroups

Usenet is a computer network accessible on the Internet that is mainly used for discussion groups. **Newsgroups** are discussion groups on Usenet organized by interest categories. Basically, newsgroups are sets of archived messages, articles, or postings. You are free to browse any newsgroup's articles.

To access newsgroups, you need a newsreader. Most graphical browsers, such as Netscape and Explorer, come equipped with a newsreader. The next thing you need to know is the Network News Transfer Protocol (NNTP) server. Contact your ISP to find out the name of its NNTP server.

Newsgroups have many **threads** of discussion. A thread is the original message that begins a discussion and all of the replies to that message. Most browsers have options for following threads. For example, when you pull up a newsgroup article in Netscape, there are links at the top of the article to all of the messages in that thread.

Newsgroup articles can literally be here today and gone tomorrow. Because of the thousands of articles a newsgroup can receive in a day, old articles are deleted to make room for the new ones.

Depending on how busy a newsgroup is, articles may be deleted within several hours. If you find an article you may want to refer to later, save or print a copy, because it may not be there the next time you look. To save a document as a file on your computer's hard drive, select Save from the File menu and choose a destination.

When accessing newsgroups, some of your basic options are to browse, read, or save newsgroup messages; to reply only to the person who posted a message or to the entire newsgroup; or to post a new message that starts a thread of discussion. Most newsreaders will have buttons for each of these options. As with listservs, it is a good idea to lurk on a newsgroup before you become an active member. To get an idea of what kinds of topics are appropriate, find out if the newsgroup has a FAQs (Frequently Asked Questions) page. Newsgroup members will become irate if you post questions that are already discussed in the FAQs, and they will not appreciate messages that discuss topics beyond the scope of their newsgroup. If you make either of these mistakes, you could get flamed—bombarded with irate mail messages! (See Info Byte: Netiquette, page 24.)

Virtual Communities: Real-Time Communication

Real-time communication is different from the various forms of delayed communication that we have discussed so far—e-mail, listservs, and newsgroups. In real time, your messages—whether text, audio, or video—are seen almost instantaneously by those on your channel, instead of being sent and read later by the recipient. There are two main methods of real-time communication—chat groups via Internet Relay Chat (**IRC**) and multi-user domains (**MUDs, MOOs, MUSHes**, etc.).

To participate in real-time communication, you need some special software. Chat groups, MUDs, MOOs, and videoconferences each require different software; sometimes, different software is even required from chat room to chat room, from MUD to MUD, and so on. This section provides an overview of some of the real-time communication options, as well as links to some Web sites to help you get started. And remember the same netiquette (see page 24) for other forms of communication is still in effect in real time. For example, avoid shouting (addressing people in all caps), and be careful not to divulge too much personal information.

Internet Relay Chat

Internet Relay Chat (IRC) is a protocol that gives you the ability to communicate in real time with people worldwide through **chat** groups. Once you have the proper software in place, you can connect to an IRC server. After you are connected to the server, you can sign on to one of the channels and communicate with others who are signed on to the same channel. You can have public conversation, where everyone on the channel is included, or a private conversation between you and one other person. Remember, though, that in IRC channels, the channel moderator can kick you off and refuse you future access, so follow netiquette.

A good place to begin is with a document called The IRC Prelude, available at <http://www.irchelp.org>. Useful software that you can download is mIRC (a graphical client) at <http://www.mirc.co.uk>. This page also provides IRC FAQs.

MUDs, MOOs, MUSHes, and WOOs

The first multi-user programming option was the Multi-User Domain (Dimension or Dungeon), or MUD. A MUD is a computer program that creates a world for users to log on to (usually by Telnet). Users can participate in role-playing, assuming various characters or personae. The next to come along were the MUD Object-Oriented environment, or MOO, and the Multi-User Shared Hallucination, or MUSH. MUDs, MOOs, MUSHes, and other multi-user domains are similar. They all have a gathering of users, usually role-playing, but MOOs and MUSHes allow for physical objects to be placed in the virtual room where the participants are gathered. The latest in multi-user technology is the Web Object-Oriented environment, or **WOO**, where Web hypermedia capabilities are combined with MOO technology. These forms of real-time communication started out as ways of facilitating multi-user games; now they are being used to create virtual societies. For beginner information, see the Daedalus Group's page at <http://www.daedalus.com/net/border.html>.

A good place to get started with multi-user options is the Pueblo site at <http://www.chaco.com/pueblo/contents.html>. Pueblo is the client software needed to participate in virtual communities; this site also provides some general information and FAQs on multi-user communities.

Videoconferencing

Videoconferencing allows you and other people around the world who are signed on to the same conference, and who have the required audio and video software and hardware, to see and hear each other. You can also show each other images and text. One of the most popular software packages for videoconferencing is CU-SeeMe. For more information on videoconferencing, including CU-SeeMe and other software, go to <http://www.rocketcharged.com/cu-seeme/>.

File Transfer Protocol (FTP)

File transfer protocol (FTP) allows you to send or retrieve files from one computer to another. In reference to the Internet, it usually means downloading files (such as text files and software programs) from the Internet to your computer. You can download huge amounts of software for free or for a minimal charge at FTP archives, such as Shareware.com at <http://www.shareware.com>.

To download a file from an FTP archive, you need to log in with a user name and password. Most FTP archives use anonymous FTP, meaning that you use the word "anonymous" as your user name and your e-mail address as your password. Browsers equipped with FTP software will do this automatically, so that when you click on a file you want to download, it will begin downloading immediately.

The Internet provides a vast number of downloadable files, such as HTML editors (used for creating Web pages), chat software, graphics animators, games (including virtual reality), and screen savers. The easiest way to find these files is to go directly to a file archive, such as Shareware.com, where you can do a key word search, search the New Arrivals, or browse Most Popular Selections (the selections downloaded most often). Much of the software is free, called **freeware.** Some software, called **shareware,** requires a small fee. (Don't let Shareware.com's name fool you; most of its software is free!) In addition to Shareware.com, a good place to find software (as well as reviews and ratings of software) is ZDNet at <http://www5.zdnet.com>.

You can search for other FTP archives by using the search engine Archie, but Archie is not as user friendly as most of the search engines we have discussed so far. With Archie, you need to know the name of the software for which you are looking. There is also a Web-based interface for using Archie, called ArchiePlex, at <http://pubweb.nexor.co.uk/public/archieplex/>. Even though ArchiePlex is Web-based, it is still rather difficult to use, so read the instructions carefully before beginning any searches.

Most graphical Web browsers, such as Netscape and Explorer, come equipped with FTP software. However, this software is usually restricted to downloading files and is not capable of sending files. In order to send files, you need full-service FTP software, which you can download for free. For the Macintosh, you can get Fetch at <http://www.dartmouth.edu/pages/softdev/fetch.html>, or for a PC, you can get a free limited version of WS_FTP at <http://www.ipswitch.com/downloads>.

Risks and Precautions

The following section deals with some of the risks that you may encounter while working with the Internet. We also suggest some precautions that may help you avoid some of the most common pitfalls.

Privacy

It is not a good idea to put anything in an e-mail message that you would not want others to see, because messages can be intercepted or sent to the wrong person. Especially if the computer you are using (or your receiver is using) belongs to your school or employer, your messages are very easy for others to access. There are privacy programs available, but using such a program may make people suspect that something secret is going on.

If you turn your computer into a server, you can have problems with individuals being able to access documents and information on your machine other than what you want to publish.

Personal Security

Sometimes you may be asked to give personal information on the Internet, especially when downloading commercial software. Reputable businesses have taken precautions to ensure the security of the information you provide. However, if you are unsure of the vendor or whenever you sign on to online news services, you should make a rule of giving just your first or last name and not giving your home address or phone number.

If you publish your own Web page (which will be discussed in Part Three), be aware that your page is accessible to the public. You want to give careful consideration to the personal information that you post on your page, such as your picture, phone numbers, and addresses. It is one thing for the whole world to have your e-mail address; it may be quite another for the whole world to be able to recognize you on sight and drive to where you live.

Copyright

It is safe to assume that most of the material on the Internet is copyrighted. The absence of a copyright notice does not mean that the material is not protected nor that it can be assumed to be in the public domain and therefore usable without seeking permission from the author or copyright holder. (For posting on the Web, however, the recommended procedure is to put "Copyright," the copyright symbol [©], the date published, the owner's name, and "All rights reserved" on documents that fall under copyright protection.) The only exception to using material from print sources that is protected by a copyright is *fair use,* which usually means reproduction of a limited amount of material for educational purposes, criticism, comment, or news reporting. However, as yet fair use has not been extended to electronic media. For more information on copyright issues, see <http://lcweb.loc.gov/copyright>.

Ideas, facts, titles, names, short phrases, and blank forms are not protected by copyright. Items in the public domain, such as government documents or items for which copyright has expired, are not protected by copyright and may be used without permission.

Libel

When someone knowingly spreads false information about another person, harming that person's reputation, or defaming them, it is called slander. However, when such information is published in print, it is defamatory writing and may be considered libelous. The same caution applies to writing published on the Web, so make sure that any information you post is true and verifiable. Libel is a crime and is punishable as a felony.

Plagiarism

For Web documents, you can create a link to someone's Web page, but you may not cut and paste any part of someone's Web page and place it on your own. Similarly, if you quote Web-page information in a written document, you must cite it properly. (See the section on documentation, starting on page 12.)

Viruses

Viruses can be devastating to your computer. They can damage or destroy both hardware and software. Viruses can get into your computer in several ways. One way is to put an infected disk into your computer's disk drive and open a file on it. Viruses can also be downloaded from the Internet when you transfer files to your computer—for example, by downloading software or text files. Viruses can also be sent via e-mail: Reading a message is not generally a problem, but if you open an attachment contaminated with a virus, your computer will become infected. Basically, if you do anything with e-mail beyond reading the message itself, your computer is susceptible to viruses.

You can detect viruses and even prevent them from contaminating your computer with virus protection software. Some computers come with anti-virus software, but you can also purchase software or download it from the Internet. For the latest on computer viruses and anti-virus software, visit the Virus Bulletin Home Page at <http://www.virusbtn.com/Welcome.html>. There you will find information such as virus names, reviews of anti-virus software, and which viruses are currently at large.

PART THREE
FINDING JOBS ON THE INTERNET

When you start looking for jobs, whether full-time, part-time, or internships, the Internet has searchable databases of job postings by employers worldwide. This use of the Internet is one of its fastest growing areas and one which is especially important for students. Depending on the kind of job you are looking for, you can search by type of job, key word, or your skills and by city, state, or country.

Sites to Search for Jobs

With services like The Career Search Launch Pad at <http://www.anet-dfw.com/~tsull/career/cslp.html>, you can access several job-search engines. The Web pages available from the Launch Pad are Career Mosaic, NationJob, Online Career Center, and Net Temps. You can access these career-search engines directly from the Launch Pad Web page, or you can link directly to each of them, using the URLs given below.

Career Mosaic <http://www.careermosaic.com>

Career Mosaic allows you to search for jobs on either the Web or Usenet by any one or any combination of

Skills description

Job title

Company name

City

State/Province

Country

Career Mosaic will sort job listings by most relevant jobs (best matches) or by most recent jobs. It will also help you get more information on top companies (browse company profiles), alert you to online job fairs, and give you access to success stories (letters from people who have used Career Mosaic). The site also includes tips on job hunting, résumé writing, and wage and salary information. Additionally, jobs can find you if you post your résumé on ResumeCM.

NationJob <http://www.nationjob.com>

NationJob allows you to search for jobs by any one or a combination of

Field (e.g., general business, engineering)

Location by U.S. region

Education (e.g., high school, bachelor's)

Job duration (full-time, part-time, temporary, or seasonal)

Salary

Key word search

Personal Job (P. J.) Scout is free and will help you search for a job; it will keep looking for jobs for you and e-mail updates on jobs that fit your qualifications. NationJob will help you get more information on companies (browse by field), find specialty job pages (browse available jobs by field), and let you read "Thank you PJ!" (success stories about using NationJob P. J.).

Online Career Center <http://www.occ.com>

Online Career Center allows you to search for jobs on the Web by any one or a combination of

Key words

City

State

With Online Career Center, you can get more information on member companies (possible employers), companies by category (industry, firms/agencies, contract, franchises), résumé writing, general career advice, corporate college recruiting, and colleges and universities.

Job Seeker Agent is free and will search for jobs for you. Each time you log on to your account, the latest jobs fitting your qualifications will be listed. Jobs can find you if you post your résumé on OCC.

Net Temps <http://www.net-temps.com>

Net Temps allows you to search for jobs on the Web by any one or a combination of

City

State

National

Net Temps will help you get more information on employers as well. If you post your résumé to Net Temps (you can post to the whole database or to a particular state), then jobs can also find you.

🖐 **Info Bit**—As you can see, many of the job-finding services allow you to post your own résumé in their databank, which can make it easier for employers who are looking for someone with your unique blend of education and experiences. Usually, for you to post your résumé you will need to have a version written in hypertext markup language (HTML). The following section (pages 32–33) on creating your own Web page will get you off to a good start in creating an HTML version of your résumé.

Internships

A great place to start looking for internships is Yahoo!'s Internships category at <http://search.yahoo.com/bin/search?p=internships>. Some of the listings are as follows:

- Anchorage Animal Hospital
  http://www.alaska.net/~animhosp

- Campus International
  http://www.internships.de/

- Center for Photography at Woodstock
  http://www.cpw.org
- Clinical Psychology Internships in the U.S. Navy
  http://members.aol.com/mcross52/psychology.html
- Construction Technology for Women
  http://www.contech.wittnn.com
- Environmental Careers Organization
  http://www.eco.org
- Explorations in Travel
  http://www.exploretravel.com
- Fund for American Studies
  http://www.dcinternships.org
- The Higher Education MoneyBook for Minorities and Women
  http://www.moneybook.com
- Independent Movie Production Jobs & Internships
  http://members.aol.com/crewjobs/
- Institute for Central American Development Studies
  http://www.icadscr.com
- International Educational Resource Center
  http://www.studyabroadierc.com
- Internships Directory from the Feminist Majority Foundation
  http://www.feminist.org/911/internship/internship.html
- JobSource
  http://www.jobsource.com
- National Internships
  http://www.internships.com/
- Rising Star Internships
  http://www.rsinternships.com
- Tripod's National Internship Directory
  http://www.tripod.com/jobs_career/intern_visa
- Washington Center for Internships and Academic Seminars
  http://www.twc.edu
- You and the Smithsonian
  http://www.si.edu/youandsi/start.htm

Scholarships

To find scholarship opportunities, go to Yahoo!'s scholarship site at <http://search.yahoo.com/search?p=scholarships>. Some of the listings are as follows:

- ExPAN Scholarship Search
  http://www.collegeboard.org/fundfinder/bin/fundfind01.pl
- fastWEB Financial Aid Search
  http://www.fastweb.com
- Rotary Foundation Ambassadorial Scholarships
  http://www.rotary.org/foundation/educational_programs
- Scholarships, Grants, & Financial Aid
  http://scholarship.vweb.net
- Scholarships for Women and Minorities
  http://members.aol.com/ox13qr/webpages/eyfswm1.html

Creating Your Own Web Pages

To post your own Web pages, you first need to make sure that your ISP has the ability to house them. There is usually an extra fee to store Web pages, so check to see what the rates are. Once you have a place to store your pages, the next step is to learn hypertext markup language (HTML). HTML uses **tags** contained in angle brackets, < >, to mark up the text of your document. Basically, HTML tags act as a set of instructions for the Web browser (such as Netscape); the tags tell the browser how your Web page should look (what's bold; what's in color; where pictures go), and how to respond to mouse clicks and keyboard strokes (if someone clicks on a link, where the browser should take them, or what Web page or file you are linking to). If you are not familiar with HTML, there is an excellent tutorial (created by Eric Meyer for Case Western University) called "Introduction to HTML." It can be found at <http://www.cwru.edu/help/introHTML/toc.html>. Also, after you start working with HTML, it's a good idea to have a cheat sheet with all the HTML tags. For such a list, go to the Bare Bones Guide for HTML 3.2 (or the most current version) by Kevin Werbach at <http://werbach.com/barebones/barebone.html>.

After you learn the basics of HTML, you can begin posting Web pages. However, you may want to refer to some style guides for creating Web pages before you begin:

- Composing Good HTML
  http://www.cs.cmu.edu/~tilt/cgh
- Elements of HTML Style (a takeoff on Strunk & White)
  http://www.book.uci.edu/Staff/StyleGuide.html
- Style Guide for Online Hypertext
  http://www.w3.org/Provider/Style/Overview.html
- Sun Microsystems's Guide to Web Style
  http://www.sun.com/styleguide
- Web Etiquette Guide
  http://www.w3.org/Provider/Style/Etiquette.html

Once you start posting Web pages, there are several key points that you should remember:

For text—

- Link to your e-mail address.
- Include a "last updated" date.
- Format text for readability.
- Do not leave any dead ends—always include a link back to your home page.
- Annotate any lists of links you include.
- Include a "Back to Top" link for long pages.

For images—

- Help minimize download time by creating small image files (**GIF** or **JPEG**).
- Use alternative text for images in case someone has disabled Auto Load Images.
- Use text links in addition to links on image maps (pictures with inserted links).

Be sure to check your page on different machines and on different browsers to make sure that it looks the way you want it to. Also, remember that the information you are posting is available to anyone, so be careful what kind of personal information you post, such as pictures, phone numbers, and addresses (see Personal Security, page 27).

Once you have your Web pages ready for the rest of the world, the final step is to make them available through search engines (such as Yahoo! or AltaVista). For other people to be able to look up your page with a search engine, you have to submit it. Of course it would be quite time-consuming to submit your page to each search engine. To help make this task easier, there is a free service called Submit It! at <http://www.submit-it.com>. Have fun!

PART FOUR
INTERNET RESOURCES

Change is inherent in the Web. As we prepared this guide, we verified every URL we listed. But by the time you read it, some of them are bound to have changed. If you follow one of our URLs and receive an error message, try typing the title of the document into your favorite search engines (such as Yahoo! or AltaVista). On the Web good things hardly ever disappear, although they do move around a lot. (Be advised that some of these services charge a user or subscription fee.) Be sure to check Part Five for specific resources related to intimacy, sexuality, and marriage and family.

Reference Material

Dictionaries and Thesauruses
- Oxford English Dictionary
  http://www.oed.com
- Roget's Thesaurus (version 1.02)
  http://www.thesaurus.com
- Webster's Revised Unabridged Dictionary, 1913 edition
  http://humanities.uchicago.edu/forms_unrest/webster.form.html
- Various dictionaries and thesauruses
  http://www.dictionary.com

Citations and Copyright
- Citation Styles for Electronic Media
  http://lamp.infosys.utas.edu.au/citation.html
- Council of Biology Editors
  http://www.cbe.org/CBE
- Electronic Sources: APA Style of Citation
  http://www.uvm.edu/~xli/reference/apa.html
- A Guide for Writing Research Papers Based on Modern Language Association
  (MLA) Documentation
  http://webster.commnet.edu/mla.htm
- IEEE
  http://www.ieee.org
- Research and Writing Guides
  http://library.scar.utoronto.ca/Bladen_Library/Bladen.html#Guides

- U.S. Copyright Office Home Page
  http://lcweb.loc.gov/copyright

- Writing Center: Chicago Style (by the University of Wisconsin-Madison)
  http://www.wisc.edu/writing/Handbook/DocChicago.html

Quotations
- Bartlett's Quotations (1901 edition)
  http://www.columbia.edu/acis/bartleby/bartlett

Libraries
- Internet Public Library
  http://ipl.sils.umich.edu

- Library of Congress
  http://lcweb.loc.gov/z3950/gateway.html#lc

News and Media

Print
- Atlantic Unbound (The Atlantic Monthly)
  http://www.theatlantic.com/index-js.htm

- The New York Times
  http://www.nytimes.com

- San Jose Mercury News
  http://www.sjmercury.com

- Time
  http://pathfinder.com/time

- USA Today
  http://www.usatoday.com

Broadcast
- CNN
  http://www.cnn.com

- MSNBC
  http://www.msnbc.com

- National Public Radio
  http://www.npr.org

- PBS
  http://www.pbs.org

- WIRED News
  http://www.wired.com

News Filters

- Pointcast (news filter/screen saver)
  http://www.pointcast.com
- CRAYON
  http://crayon.net

Books and Book Reviews

- Amazon.com
  http://www.amazon.com
- BookWire (*Publishers Weekly* Web page, including best-seller lists)
  http://www.bookwire.com
- Borders on the Web
  http://www.borders.com
- Dial-A-Book Chapter One
  http://www1.psi.net/chapterone
- The Independent Reader (leading booksellers' recommendations)
  http://www.independentreader.com
- Salon Magazine
  http://www.salonmagazine.com

Online Writing Centers

- The Alliance for Computers and Writing (Comprehensive—the only one you'll really need.)
  http://english.ttu.edu/acw/acw.html
- A Guide for Writing Research Papers (Excellent interactive grammar tutorials.)
  http://webster.commnet.edu/mla.htm
- Paradigm Online Writing Assistant
  http://www.idbsu.edu/english/cguilfor/paradigm

People Finders

- BigFoot
  http://www.bigfoot.com
- Four11
  http://www.four11.com
- InfoSpace
  http://www.infospace.com
- Netscape's White Pages (Community building)
  http://home.netscape.com/escapes/whitepages/community.html

- Switchboard
  http://www.switchboard.com
- WhoWhere?
  http://www.whowhere.com

Cool Stuff

- c|net (A Web surfing must—something for everyone.)
  http://www.cnet.com
- The Discovery Channel
  http://www.discovery.com
- IPIX (Download IPIX's immersive image plugin and take virtual tours of places like the space shuttle and Chicago's Field Museum.)
  http://www.ipix.com
- MTV (Most everything from videos to music news.)
  http://www.mtv.com
- Mag's Big List of HTML Editors (If you know HTML and wish you had an editor to help, this list will have something for you.)
  http://www.davis.k12.ut.us/knowlton/LDSBC/webclass/editors.htm
- Mapquest (Find places, plan the routes for your trips, and don't forget to try the interactive world atlas.)
  http://www.mapquest.com/
- Megabyte University Discussion List (Find out more about MUDs, MOOs, etc.)
  http://www.daedalus.com/MBU/MBU.intro.html
- Netscape Plugins (Browse the different and mostly free components that you can download and add to your Netscape browser, such as audio, video, and animation software.)
  http://home.netscape.com/comprod/products/navigator/version_2.0/plugins/html
- The Virtual Library of Museums (Browse museums by country, by exhibition, or by special interest; even contains virtual tours.)
  http://www.comlab.ox.ac.uk/archive/other/museums.html
- Yahoo!'s Games (Yahoo!'s directory of fun and games.)
  http://www.yahoo.com/Recreation/Games

Sites for Teachers

- Editor & Publisher Home Page
  http://www.mediainfo.com
- The National Writing Centers Association Page
  http://departments.colgate.edu/NWCA.html

- THE SLOT: A Spot for Copy Editors
  http://www.theslot.com
- Workshops for Copy Editors in Book and Magazine Publishing
  http://www.copyeditor.com/BookMagazineWorkshops.html
- World Lecture Hall
  http://www.utexas.edu/world/lecture
- Writing Across the Curriculum Guide (Bibliography)
  http://orchard.cortland.edu/WACguide/WACsection2.html

Newsgroups

Newsgroups have specific notations for different kinds of discussion groups to help in organizing Usenet's hierarchical structure. These categories are the following:

bionet	biology
biz	business
ClariNet	news feeds
comp	computers
k12	education
misc	miscellaneous
news	Usenet info
rec	hobbies, sports
sci	general science
soc	social topics
talk	anything
alt	alternative newsgroups

Some Newsgroups for Students
- alt.education.student.government
- alt.humor.best-of-usenet
- alt.journalism.students
- rec.music.makers.songwriting
- soc.college.gradinfo

Some Newsgroups for Teachers
- alt.books.reviews
- alt.education
- misc.writing

PART FIVE
INTERNET RESOURCES FOR INTIMACY, SEXUALITY, AND MARRIAGE AND THE FAMILY

Introduction

This collection of resources serves as a starting point for finding resources on the World Wide Web. These sites represent only a small sample of the resources available at merely one time in an environment that is constantly changing. New pages are continually being added, just as existing pages are being modified or becoming outdated or extinct. We tried to include those Web pages supported by fairly prominent and stable organizations in the fields of human sexuality, marriage and the family, and psychology. In addition, we included references to Web sites that showed evidence of regular upkeep, to better ensure access to current information.

Web resources are presented in ten sections. For each section, we tried to provide a variety of sites that offer different types of resources or that approach the same topic from different perspectives. A brief description of the site accompanies each Web page listing. Some sections also include Web Exercises that offer select Web resources related to a central topic of interest. These exercises should help you think critically about the subject material as you consider information from more than one source. These exercises also should facilitate your exploration of the Web and allow you to discover some interesting sites on your own.

Popular Culture and the Media: Images and Distortions

- Asian Rose Travel & Tours <http://www.freeyellow.com/members2/asianrose/index.html>
  This Web page provides information regarding escorted tours to the Philippines and other locations in Asia for the purpose of "gentlemen clients" meeting "marriage-minded ladies."

- Communication Studies: Gender & Race in Media
  <http://www.uiowa.edu/~commstud/resources/GenderMedia.html>
  This Web site contains critical essays regarding media depictions based on gender, sexual orientation, and race and ethnicity (including African American, Asian American, Latin American, and Native American populations). It covers different forms of media including advertising, cyberspace, print media, television and film, and mixed media.

- Cyber Romance 101 <http://web2.airmail.net/walraven/romance.htm>
  This Web site provides information regarding relationships forged on the Internet. Essays (both personal and theoretical), fiction, and other resources are provided that address the implications of cyber-relationships and how technological advances affect the ways in which relationships are defined.

- Dating and Relationships <http://www.netadssell.com/dating/>
  This site is a listing of dating and relationship links on the Internet. These links are mostly dating services or forums for finding a mate.

- Internet Indecency and Communications Decency Act
  <http://www.gslis.utexas.edu/~cjyoung/index.html>
  This page provides research surrounding the Communications Decency Act of 1996, presenting links to organizations on both sides of the debate.

- The Internet Personals <http://www.montagar.com/personals/index.html>
  This site allows you to publish your own personal ad on the World Wide Web. Both browsing and placing ads are free. The site includes a searchable database based on age, geographic location, and personal preferences.

- Sex, Censorship, and the Internet <http://www.eff.org/CAF/cafuiuc.html>
  This site offers a discussion of academic freedom and scientific inquiry as it relates to issues of sexuality.

- The Sexuality of Elderly People in Film: Visual Limitations
  <http://www.soc.uu.se/research/gerontology/tb_abstract.html>
  This Web page contains an essay regarding cultural representations of aging and sexuality as reflected in film. It also contains links to related sites.

- SIECUS Fact Sheets: Media Recommendations for More Realistic, Accurate Images Concerning Sexuality <http://www.siecus.org/pubs/fact/fact0004.html>
  This site presents a statement, endorsed by the National Coalition to Support Sexuality Education, that encourages media professionals to use more realistic, accurate images concerning sexuality.

- The Swoon Personals <http://personals.swoon.com/e_personals/personals.html>
  This site offers free access to classified personal ads. It allows advanced searches based on gender, age, ethnicity, religion, location by area code, marital status, educational level, physical characteristics, and social preferences (smoking, drinking, and drugs).

Web Exercise: Personal Ads and the Making of a Relationship
A. Visit the following Web sites and browse the personal ads:

- The Internet Personals <http://www.montagar.com/personals/index.html>

- The Swoon Personals <http://personals.swoon.com/e_personals/personals.html>

    1. If you were searching for a partner, what personal characteristics would you use as criteria for your search? Why would these characteristics be important to you?

    2. Would these characteristics differ if you wanted to (a) develop a friendship, (b) find a date, or (c) develop a long-term relationship? If so, how?

3. How does defining a partner in the context of a personal ad relate to your own definition of a relationship?

4. What information would you include in your own personal ad?

5. How would the information you provide about yourself relate to your own definition of a relationship?

B. Browse the following Web sites and think about the different ways in which relationships are defined:

- Asian Rose Travel & Tours <http://www.freeyellow.com/members2/asianrose/index.html>
- Cyber Romance 101 <http://web2.airmail.net/walraven/romance.htm>

Web Exercise: Sexuality and Censorship on the Internet

A. Browse the following Web sites to the extent that your interest and comfort levels, as well as your age, allow. (There are age restrictions for viewing some of this material.) For each site, note how images of sexuality are presented and describe your own feelings or reactions to these images.

- Alchemy Mindworks: Indecent Images <http://www.mindworkshop.com/alchemy/ indcnt.html>. This site presents a collection of pre-Raphaelite paintings.
- Good Vibrations <http://www.goodvibes.com/>. This online store offers sex toys, videos, information about sexual health, and an antique vibrator museum.
- Sex etc.: A Webpage by Teens for Teens <http://www.rci.rutgers.edu/~sxetc/>. This Web site is dedicated to the discussion of sexuality and relationships for teens.
- Sexhunter <http://www.last-hope.com/huntera/>. This Web address will link you to the introductory (cautionary) page to pornographic Web sites. To enter, you must agree to accept an adult site membership. This page describes membership terms and the benefits of membership.
- SOLO <http://www.proaxis.com/~solo/>. This Web page is devoted to providing educational information about human sexuality with particular emphasis on masturbation.

1. What do all of these sites have in common?

2. Think about the collective information from these sites. What would be *lost* if these types of sites were successfully censored?

3. Again, think about the collective information from these sites. What would be *gained* if these types of Web sites were successfully censored?

4. How does the collective representation of sexual material affect our understanding of sexual issues and sexual norms?

5. How does the material relate to our images of sexuality across gender, race and ethnicity, class, and sexual orientation?

B. Visit the following Web sites and read more about both sides of the censorship debate:

- Internet Indecency and Communications Decency Act
  <http://www.gslis.utexas.edu/~cjyoung/index.html>
- Sex, Censorship, and the Internet <http://www.eff.org/CAF/cafuiuc.html>

Sources of Scientific Information

Organizations

- American Association for Marriage and Family Therapy (AAMFT) <http://www.aamft.org>
  This Web page includes information regarding membership, accreditation, and the association's annual conference. Selected articles are available from AAMFT's newsletter *Family Therapy News*. Users can also access abstracts and tables of contents for the *Journal of Marital and Family Therapy*.

This Web site also includes a listing of student resources, including student membership and career and internship information.

- American Association of Sex Educators, Counselors, and Therapists (AASECT)
  <http://www. aasect.org/>
  This Web page includes a mission statement, membership information, and publication information for the journals *Contemporary Sexuality* and the *Journal of Sex Education and Therapy Quarterly.*

- American Psychological Association (APA) <http://www.apa.org>.
  This Web page includes a description of the organization, membership criteria, job and internship opportunities, information for all APA journals, and a search engine for the APA journal database. Information regarding student membership is also available.

- American Psychological Society (APS) <http://www.hanover.edu/psych/APS/aps.html>.
  This Web page includes information on the organization and publications including the *Observer.* This Web site also links to the APS Student Caucus, which provides information on membership; conferences; and student grants, awards, and travel funds. It also offers a job resource guide.

- The Kinsey Institute for Research in Sex, Gender, and Reproduction
  <http://www.indiana.edu/~kinsey/>.
  This Web page includes information on institute activities and the history of sexology. It also includes links to recommended journals and professional organizations.

- The National Council on Family Relations (NCFR) <http://www.ncfr.com/body.html>.
  This Web page includes a brief description of the organization as well as contact information. NCFR publishes two scholarly journals: *Journal of Marriage and the Family* and *Family Relations.* (Direct URLs are given for these journals in the subsection "Journals: Marriage and Relationship Issues," which follows.)

- Sexuality Information and Education Council of the United States (SIECUS)
  <http://www.siecus.org/>.
  This Web page contains articles on current controversies and research in the field, in addition to information about the organization itself. It serves as an important resource for parents, students, and researchers.

- The Society for the Scientific Study of Sexuality (SSSS) <http://www.ssc.wisc.edu/ssss/>.
  This Web page includes information regarding society membership, conference announcements and publications (including a table of contents for the *Annual Review of Sex Research* and *The Journal of Sex Research*). The site also includes program listings for educational opportunities in human sexuality.

- World Association for Sexology (WAS) <http://www.tc.umn.edu/nlhome/m201/colem001/was/>.
  WAS works to promote international and intercultural exchange of scientific information of sexology. This Web page describes the association's objectives, provides membership information, and offers resources, including Web links.

Journals: Human Sexuality Issues

Most of the journal listings contain contact and subscription information, and a table of contents for recent issues. A few of the links contain abstracts or full text for selected articles.

- *Annual Review of Sex Research* <http://www.ssc.wisc.edu/ssss/annual_review.htm>.
  Contact and subscription information, table of contents.
- *Archives of Sexual Behavior* <http://www.plenum.com/title.cgi?2069>.
  Contact and subscription information, table of contents.
- *The International Journal of Transgenderism* <http://www.symposion.com/ijt/index.htm>.
  Contact and subscription information, table of contents, full text for articles.
- *Journal of Gay and Lesbian Social Services* <http://www.haworthpressinc.com>.
  Contact and subscription information, table of contents.
- *Journal of Gay, Lesbian, and Bisexual Identity* <http://www.plenum.com/title.cgi?1045>.
  Contact and subscription information, table of contents.
- *Journal of Homosexuality* <http://www.haworthpressinc.com>.
  Contact and subscription information, table of contents.
- *Journal of Psychology & Human Sexuality* <http://www.haworthpressinc.com>.
  Contact and subscription information, table of contents.
- *Journal of Sex and Marital Therapy* <http://www.tandfdc/JNLS/smt.htm>.
  Contact and subscription information, table of contents.
- *The Journal of Sex Research* <http://www.ssc.wisc.edu/ssss/jsr.htm>.
  Contact and subscription information, table of contents.
- *Sexual & Marital Therapy* <http://www.carfax.co.uk/smi-ad.htm>.
  Contact and subscription information, table of contents.
- *Sexualities: Studies in Culture and Society* <http://www.sagepub.co.uk/journals/details/j0065.html>.
  Contact and subscription information, table of contents.
- *Sexuality and Disability* <http://www.plenum.com/title.cgi?1035>.
  Contact and subscription information, table of contents.
- *Violence Against Women* <http://www.sagepub.co.uk/journals/details/j0062.html>.
  Contact and subscription information, table of contents.

Journals: Marriage and Relationship Issues

Most of the journal listings contain contact and subscription information and a table of contents for recent issues. A few of the links contain abstracts or full text for selected articles.

- *American Journal of Family Therapy* <http://www.tandfdc.com/JNLS/AFT.htm>.
  Contact and subscription information, table of contents.
- *Child Abuse & Neglect* <http://www.elsevier.nl:80/inca/publications/store/5/8/6>.
  Contact and subscription information.

- *Child and Family Social Work* <http://www.uea.ac.uk/swk/publicat/cfsw.htm>
  Contact and subscription information, table of contents.
- *Community, Work & Family* <http://www.carfax.co.uk/cwf-ad.htm>
  Contact and subscription information, table of contents.
- *Contemporary Family Therapy* <http://www.plenum.com/title.cgi?1010>
  Contact and subscription information, table of contents.
- *The Family Journal: Counseling and Therapy for Couples and Families*
  <http://familycounselors.org/pubs.html>
  Contact and subscription information.
- *Family Process* <http://www.familyprocess.org>
  Contact and subscription information.
- *Family Relations* <http://www.iog.wayne.edu/FR/homepage.html>
  Contact and subscription information.
- *Journal of Child and Family Studies* <http://www.plenum.com/title.cgi?1042>
  Contact and subscription information, table of contents.
- *Journal of Child Sexual Abuse* <http://www.haworthpressinc.com>
  Contact and subscription information, table of contents.
- *Journal of Couples Therapy* <http://www.haworthpressinc.com>
  Contact and subscription information, table of contents.
- *Journal of Divorce & Remarriage* <http://www.haworthpressinc.com>
  Contact and subscription information, table of contents.
- *Journal of Family Issues* <http://www.sagepub.co.uk/journals/details/j0179.html>
  Contact and subscription information.
- *Journal of Family Psychology* <http://www.apa.org:80/journals/fam.html>
  Contact and subscription information, table of contents, abstracts.
- *Journal of Family Violence* <http://www.plenum.com/title.cgi?2044>
  Contact and subscription information, table of contents.
- *Journal of Feminist Family Therapy* <http://www.haworthpressinc.com>
  Contact and subscription information, table of contents.
- *Journal of Interpersonal Violence* <http://www.sagepub.co.uk/journals/details/j0015.html>
  Contact and subscription information.
- *Journal of Marital and Family Therapy* <http://www.aamft.org/resources/jmft_menu.htm>
  Contact and subscription information, table of contents, abstracts, full text for selected articles.
- *Journal of Marriage and the Family* <http://www.ncfr.com/jour_intro.html>
  Contact and subscription information.
- *Journal of Sex and Marital Therapy* <http://www.tandfdc.com/JNLS/smt.htm>
  Contact and subscription information, table of contents.

- *Marriage & Family Review* <http://www.haworthpressinc.com>
  Contact and subscription information, table of contents.
- *Sexual & Marital Therapy* <http://www.carfax.co.uk/smt-ad.htm>
  Contact and subscription information, table of contents.
- *Studies in Family Planning* <http://www.popcouncil.org/sfp/>
  Contact and subscription information, table of contents, abstracts.

Forums

- Community of Science Web Server <http:www.cos.com>
  This Web site is a scientific database of researchers and academics. Searches can be conducted by name, area of expertise, and region of the country.
- Network for Family Life Education <http://rasputin-cscd.rutgers.edu/nfleover.htm>
  This network of agencies has joined to support family life and human sexuality education in school and community settings. The Web site includes information about publications, videos, conferences, and workshops. It also includes a link to "Sex etc.," a Web page by teens for teens about love, sex, relationships, abstinence, contraception, AIDS, STDs, and other topics related to sexuality.
- PsychCrawler <http://www.psychcrawler.com/plweb>
  PsychCrawler is supported by the American Psychological Association and is a search engine for journal articles in psychology.
- Psychology Web Pointer <http://www.grohol.com/web.htm>
  Dr. John Grohol's Mental Health Page, Psychology Web Pointer, allows access to World Wide Web pages associated with mental health, psychology, and support resources. References are organized into three alphabetized categories: general resources, professional resources, and other resource lists. Each category contains detailed descriptions for each link.
- PsychREF: Resources in Psychology on the Internet
  <http://maple.lemoyne.edu/~hevern/ psychref.html>
  This index of resources for faculty and students in psychology includes resources specifically for students as well as lists for different subfields in psychology. It is geared toward academic use.
- Psych Web <http://www.psych-web.com>
  This searchable database offers psychology-related resources for students and teachers of psychology. It includes both scholarly and self-help resources, Web links, discussion pages, and information about careers in psychology.
- PsycSite Home <http://stange.simplenet.com/psycsite/html>
  This searchable resource focuses on the science of psychology rather than on treatment or self-help.
- Sex Education Resources on the World-Wide Web
  <http://www.jagunet.com/~dgotlib/ meanstreets.htm>
  This updated list of sex education resources is geared toward academic and medical treatment resources. It includes information on a variety of sexual disorders and links to professional sex journals and organizations.

- Sexology Netline <http://home.netinc.ca/~sexorg/index.htm>
  This Web site is sponsored by the Institute for Advanced Study of Human Sexuality and contains fact sheets on various topics related to sex. It also includes a question-and-answer section as well as standard references and resources.

- Sexual Health Network <http://www.sexualhealth.com/>
  This Web site is a directory of information and resources regarding sexuality, education, counseling, and therapy for people with disabilities, illnesses, or other health-related problems. It includes a discussion board and related links.

Web Exercise: Finding Information on the Web
Use this exercise to find information and resources on the Web related to a course topic of interest to you.

1. State the topic of your research paper or class project.

2. Generate and list key words that reflect your topic of interest. You will use these words to identify documents in a database that are related to your topic. They should be fairly specific, to limit the number of documents identified and to ensure that you are finding documents that are most relevant to your topic.

3. Search using a psychology database rather than a general search engine. You will be more likely to find relevant and reliable sources of information. Access the following three psychology databases and perform a search using your identified key words. Note the number and types of links generated by each search.

    • PsychCrawler <http://www.psychcrawler.com/plweb/>

    • PsycSite Home <http://stange.simplenet.com/psycsite/html>

    • Psych Web <http://www.psych-web.com/>

4. If you cannot find the information you are looking for, you may want to run similar searches by varying your key words and noting the differences in the documents found. List other useful Web sites you find.

5. Once you identify information to be used in your research, be sure that you are aware of the proper way to cite documents retrieved from the World Wide Web. Use the guidelines from the American Psychological Association, available at "How to Cite Information from the Internet and the World Wide Web," <http://www.apa.org/journals/webref.html> and the information in Part One of this guide.

Cultural Diversities on Love, Sex, and Marriage: A World of Difference

- African American Resources <http://scuish.scu.edu/SCU/Programs/Diversity/african.html>
  Sponsored by Santa Clara University, this Web page provides Web resources, links to electronic journals, reference materials, and scholarly resources related to African American issues.

- American Indian Institute <http://www.occe.ou.edu/aii/>
  This Web page provides information and events for the institute. It also links to many organizations and Web pages regarding Native American research and history, service agencies, and education.

- APA Division 45: Society for the Psychological Study of Ethnic Minority Issues
  <http:www.apa.org/about/division.html#d45>
  Division 45 supports a discussion list for topics relevant to ethnic minority issues. Additional information is available through the APA home page <http://www.apa.org>

- Asian American Studies Resources
  <http://www.lib.uci.edu/home/collect/interdis/asamer.html>
  This Web page contains links to articles, research institutes, and organizations related to Asian Americans.

- Building Chicana/o Latina/o Communities Through Networking
  <http://latino.sscnet.ucla.edu>
  This site provides information related to Chicano and Latino issues including health, sexuality, and literature. It also contains a research center that organizes documents by discipline. A separate site provides information related specifically to Chicana/Latina issues: <http://clnet.ucr.edu/women/womenHP.html>.

- Center for World Indigenous Studies <http://www.halcyon.com/FWDP/cwisinfo.html>
  This site contains the archives from the Center for World Indigenous Studies, a nonprofit research and educational organization. The Web site allows access to archival records affecting indigenous peoples in North and South America, Africa, Asia, Europe, and the Pacific Islands.

- Communication Studies: Gender & Race in Media
  <http://www.uiowa.edu/~commstud/resources/GenderMedia.html>
  This Web site contains critical essays regarding media depictions based on gender, sexual orientation, and race and ethnicity (including African American, Asian American, Latin American, and Native American populations). The site covers different forms of media including advertising, print media, television and film, Web-based media, and mixed media.

- Diversity & Ethnic Studies: Virtual Community
  <http://www.public.iastate.edu/~savega/divweb2.htm>
  This Web site provides bibliographies and links for resources that relate to African Americans, American Indians, Asian Americans, and U.S. Latinos and Latinas. It also contains information for other forms of diversity based on sexual orientation and disability.

- International Planned Parenthood Federation (IPPF) <http://www.ippf.org/>
  This Web page provides information about IPPF, as well as a discussion on the need for family planning and the status of sexual and reproductive rights internationally. It also provides contact information for regional associations.

- Interracial Voice <http://www.webcom.com/intvoice>
  This bimonthly news journal for the interracial community in cyberspace presents articles, book reviews, and relevant news stories.

- Society for Cross-Cultural Research (SCCR)
  <http://www.fit.edu/CampusLife/clubs-org/sccr/index.html>
  This Web page offers general information about the organization, as well as the SCCR newsletter and table of contents for recent issues of the journal *Cross-Cultural Research.*

- World Association for Sexology (WAS) <http://www.tc.umn.edu/nlhome/m201/colem001/was/>
  The World Association for Sexology works to promote international and intercultural exchange of scientific information on sexology. This Web page describes the association's objectives, provides membership information, and includes reference information and related Web links.

Sexual Orientations: The Many Expressions of Close and Intimate Relationships

- Answers to Your Questions About Sexual Orientation and Homosexuality
  <http://www.apa.org/pubinfo/orient.html>
  This Web site is published by the American Psychological Association.

- APA Division 44: Society for the Psychological Study of Lesbian, Gay, and Bisexual Issues
  <http://www.apa.org/about/division.html#d44>
  Additional information is available through the APA home page.

- Children of Lesbians and Gays Everywhere (COLAGE) <http://www.COLAGE.org/>
  COLAGE is a support and advocacy organization for daughters and sons of lesbian, gay, bisexual, and transgender parents. The Web site contains membership information as well as related resources and links.

- Gay and Lesbian National Hotline (GLNH) <http://www.glnh.org/>
  This Web site provides information about the GLNH including hours and available services. It also provides crisis-related information for gay men and lesbians, related links, and local switchboard and community center information.

- Gay & Lesbian Parents Coalition International (GLPCI) <http://www.glpci.org/>
  This site provides information, support, and activist resources concerning lesbian, gay, bisexual, and transgender parents.

- Lesbian and Gay Parenting <http://www.apa.org/pi/parent.html>
  This link contains the APA published statement regarding lesbian and gay parenting.

- National Consortium of Directors of LGBT Resources in Higher Education
  <http://www.uic.edu/orgs/lgbt/index.html>
  This Web page provides information about the organization and a directory of links to LGBT campus offices and centers.

- National Organization of Gay and Lesbian Scientists and Technical Professionals
  <http://www.noglstp.org>
  This site contains information about the professional organization. It also contains links to other organizations and Web resources.

- Parents, Families, and Friends of Lesbians and Gays (PFLAG) <http://www.pflag,org>.
  PFLAG is a national organization that provides support and resources for parents, families, and friends of lesbians and gays. The Web page contains organization information, news items, project information (including Internet workshops), publications and fact sheets, an online store, and a directory of Web links for regional PFLAG chapters.

- Queer Resources Directory <http://www.qrd.org/>
  This comprehensive directory connecting organizations and resources is arranged by subject headings that cover family, health, religion, and youth issues, among others.

- Sexual Orientation: Science, Education, and Policy
  <http://psychology.ucdavis.edu/rainbow/index.html>
  This Web page was designed by psychologist Dr. Gregory Herek. It surveys the scientific data on issues related to sexual orientation. Information regarding homophobia, AIDS, and lesbian and gay stereotypes is available.

Web Exercise: Sexual Orientation and the Family

Browse the resources found at the following two Web sites:

- Children of Lesbian and Gays Everywhere (COLAGE) <http://www.COLAGE.org/>

- Parents, Families, and Friends of Lesbians and Gays (PFLAG) <http://www.pflag.org>

    1. What unique challenges do children of lesbian, gay, bisexual, or transgender (LGBT) persons face? Why?

2. What unique challenges do parents of lesbian, gay, bisexual, or transgender persons face?

3. What information contained on each of the Web pages surprised you? Why?

4. How do the following issues concerning sexual orientation relate to our traditional notion of family and relationships?
    a. Lesbians, gay men, and bisexuals as parents

    b. Lesbian and gay couples

    c. Same-sex marriage

5. How do the terms *sexual orientation* and *affectional orientation* relate to our notion of family, relationships, and marriage?

6. In the LGBT community, it is commonplace to refer to other LGBT persons as "family." After reading about the experiences of lesbians, gay men, bisexuals, and transgendered persons, explain why this word usage may have developed.

A Gendered World: Feminist and Masculinist Perspectives on Relationships

- APA Division 35: Psychology of Women <http://www.apa.org/about/division.html#d35>
  This Web page includes a mission statement; contact information; and information on publications, special interest groups, projects, and awards.

- APA Division 51: The Society for the Psychological Study of Men and Masculinity <http://web.indstate.edu/spsmm>
  This feminist organization is devoted to understanding the changing roles of men.

- Feminist.com <http://www.feminist.com/>
  This Web page offers the Washington Feminist Faxnet (created by the Center for Advancement of Public Policy), a weekly report on current policy items from Washington, D.C. The report provides weekly news items and updates on policy issues and legislation affecting women. Feminist.com houses numerous women's not-for-profit organizations.

- The Feminist Majority Foundation Online <http://www.feminist.org/>
  This site is a major resource for feminist information on the Internet. It includes current news items, news on legislative action, and resources on issues related to feminism, arranged by topic.

- MensNet <http://infoweb.magi.com/~mensnet/>
  MensNet is a network for "pro-feminist, gay affirmative, anti-racist, male positive men." The Web site includes a library of information and articles on topics related to men, gender, politics, men's role in feminism, and male sexuality, among others.

- National Coalition of Free Men (NCFM) <http://www.ncfm.org/>
  NCFM is a nonprofit educational organization devoted to the study of how sex discrimination affects men.

- National Organization for Women (NOW) <http:/www.now.org>
  NOW is a feminist organization that focuses on issues affecting women, including abortion and reproductive rights, affirmative action, economic equality, and violence against women.

- The World Wide Web Virtual Library: The Men's Issues Page <http://www.vix.com/men/index.html>
  This collection of resources relates to the various men's movements and includes contact information and Web pages for men's organizations. The index is organized by topic. (Topics include domestic violence, false rape and abuse, fatherhood and single dad issues, and marriage and relationships.)

Sexual Health and Well-Being

- American Social Health Association <http://sunsite.unc.edu/ASHA/main/main.html>
  The mission of this association is to stop the spread of sexually transmitted diseases (STDs) and to educate individuals, families, and communities of the harmful consequences of STDs. This Web page includes a sexual health glossary, STD information, educational materials, news on legislative actions, and support group information.

- Center for AIDS Prevention Studies (CAPS) <http://www.caps.ucsf.edu/capsweb/index. html>
  This Web page contains information regarding CAPS. It also provides information regarding general

HIV prevention information, program evaluation, methodological concerns for HIV prevention studies, fact sheets, and related links.

- Go Ask Alice! <http://www.goaskalice.columbia.edu/index.html>
  This health-related question-and-answer service, sponsored by Columbia University, includes advice about sexuality, sexual health, relationships, alcohol and drug use, fitness and nutrition, emotional well-being, and general health.

- The Kinsey Institute for Research in Sex, Gender, and Reproduction
  <http://www.indiana.edu/~kinsey/>
  This Web page includes information on institute activities and the history of sexology. It also includes links to recommended journals and professional organizations.

- Sex Education Resources on the World-Wide Web: Recommended Sites
  <http://www.jagunet.com/~dgotlib/meanstreets.htm>
  This updated list of sex education resources is geared toward academic and medical treatment resources. It includes information on a variety of sexual disorders and links to professional sex journals and organizations.

- Sexual Health InfoCenter <http://www.sexhealth.org/infocenter/infomain.htm>
  This site contains information and links related to better sex, safer sex, STDs, sexuality and aging, LGBT issues, and sexual problems. It also provides a forum for answering questions related to sexual health.

- Sexual Health Network <http://www.sexualhealth.com/>
  This Web site is a directory of information and resources regarding sexuality, education, counseling, and therapy for people with disabilities, illnesses, or other health-related problems. It includes a discussion board and related links.

- SOLO <http://www.proaxis.com/~solo/>
  This Web page is devoted to providing educational information about human sexuality with particular emphasis on masturbation. It provides information on the latest research about masturbation from both medical and psychological perspectives.

Reproductive Decisions, Contraception, and Family Planning

- Access to Voluntary and Safe Contraception (AVSC) International
  <http://www.avsc.org/avsc/index.html>
  AVSC International engages in a worldwide effort to improve reproductive health services. This Web page offers information about contraception, the role of informed choice in contraceptive issues, infections and diseases, gender issues in contraceptive decision making, and family planning services.

- Contraception Links <http://www-hsl.mcmaster.ca/tomflem/backup/contracep.html>
  This site is a compilation of contraception links by Health Care Information Resources (McMaster University).

- Emergency Contraception Web site <http://opr.princeton.edu/ec/>
  This site provides information about research related to emergency contraceptive methods. It also includes recent publications and news items as well as a directory of providers.

- Family Health International (FHI) <http://www.fhi.org>
  FHI is invested in the study and improvement of reproductive health around the world, especially in developing countries. This Web site contains a searchable database and resources and links for family planning; HIV, AIDS, and STDs; and women's studies.

- Family Planning Advocates of New York State (FPA) and the Education Fund of Family Planning Advocates <http://www.fpaofnys.org/>
  This New York-based advocacy group aims to ensure women's reproductive freedom. This Web site contains information about the organization; news about legislative actions in New York; and fact sheets on the mission of the FPA, family planning and welfare policies, family planning and at-risk populations, sexually transmitted infections, teen pregnancies, and responsible sexuality education.

- International Planned Parenthood Federation (IPPF) <http://www.ippf.org/>
  This Web page provides information about IPPF, as well as a discussion on the need for family planning and the status of sexual and reproductive rights internationally. It provides contact information for regional associations.

- The International Professional Surrogates Association (IPSA)
  <http://members.aol.com/Ipsa1/home.html>
  IPSA is an educational organization for the profession of surrogate partners. The Web page provides information about IPSA as well as educational, therapeutic, ethical, and legal issues related to surrogate partners and therapists.

- National Abortion and Reproductive Rights Action League: NARAL On-Line
  <http://www. naral.org>
  This site offers press releases, publications, news reports, and action items. This page also contains links to state affiliates and campus organizations of NARAL.

- National Mental Health and Education Center for Children and Families
  <http://www.naspweb.org/center.html>
  The center is a public service program sponsored by the National Association of School Psychologists. Its Web page contains information for parents, teachers, and educators.

- The Official Condom Directory <http://users.deltanet.com/~agkid/>
  This page serves as a directory for Web sites related to condoms. These sites are supported mainly by condom retailers or manufacturers, most of which provide educational information about the use of condoms for contraceptive and safe-sex purposes.

- Planned Parenthood <http://www.plannedparenthood.org/main.html>
  This on-line source of sexual and reproductive health information allows viewers to input their local zip codes in order to access localized information.

- Population Council <http://www.popcouncil.org/>
  This Web page contains a mission statement for the council, and descriptions of programs, publications, and sponsored research. Job opportunities and Web resources also are listed.

Developing and Maintaining Relationships

- alt.polyamory <http://www.polyamory.org/>
  This is the home page for the Usenet newsgroup <alt.polyamory>. It contains links to organizations and resources addressing polyamory from an interdisciplinary perspective (law, sociology, psychology, and biology). It also includes personals, essays, and newsgroup excerpts.

- Cyber Romance 101 <http://web2.airmail.net/walraven/romance.htm>
  This Web site provides information regarding relationships forged on the Internet. Essays (both personal and theoretical), fiction, and other resources are provided that address the implications of cyber-relationships and how technological advances affect the ways in which relationships are defined.

- Go Ask Alice! <http://www.goaskalice.columbia.edu/index.html>
  This health-related question-and-answer service is sponsored by Columbia University. It includes advice about sexuality, sexual health, relationships, alcohol and drug use, fitness and nutrition, emotional well-being, and general health.

- Grandparents, Brothers & Sisters
  <http://www.personal.psu.edu/faculty/n/x/nxd10/extended.htm#top>
  This Web site contains essays from students at Penn State on issues of family relationships between grandparents and siblings. These essays are short but provide a good overview of each topic as well as relevant references.

- Intimate Relationships . . . from dating through divorce
  <http://www.personal.psu.edu/faculty/n/x/nxd10/relation.htm#top>
  This Web site contains essays from students at Penn State on issues related to intimate relationships. Topics include dating and sexuality, communication, living as partners, breaking up, and lesbian and gay relationships. These essays are short but provide a good overview of each topic as well as relevant references.

- Loving More <http://www.lovemore.com/>
  This quarterly magazine is designed to support, explore, and enhance responsibility in relationships. It promotes a diversity of legitimate options for intimacy, sexuality, and family life including monogamy and responsible polyamory (including all forms of ethical and consensual multipartner relations between adults).

Therapy and Enrichment: From Medical Help to Counseling

- American Medical Association (AMA) <http://www.ama-assn.org/>
  This Web site offers information for physicians as well as the general public. It includes a Doctor Finder and a Hospital Finder and allows a search of medical news and specific medical conditions. Full text articles are available for some medical journals.

- American Social Health Association <http://sunsite.unc.edu/ASHA/main/main.html>
  The mission of this association is to stop the spread of sexually transmitted diseases (STDs) and to educate individuals, families, and communities to the harmful consequences of STDs. This Web page

includes a sexual health glossary, STD information, educational materials, news on legislative actions, and support group information.

- Family Health International (FHI) <http://www.fhi.org>
  FHI is invested in the study and improvement of reproductive health around the world, especially in developing countries. This Web site contains a searchable database and resources and links for family planning; HIV, AIDS, and STDs; and women's studies.

- Go Ask Alice! <http://www.goaskalice.columbia.edu/index.html>
  This health-related question-and-answer service is sponsored by Columbia University. It includes advice about sexuality, sexual health, relationships, alcohol and drug use, fitness and nutrition, emotional well-being, and general health.

- Internet Mental Health <http://www.mentalhealth.com/main.html>
  This site contains basic information regarding mental health disorders, associated medications, and diagnoses.

- Mental Health Net <http://www.cmhc.com/>
  This site lists more than 7000 resources related to mental health, psychology, and psychiatry. It offers professional resources and information regarding disorders and treatments.

Violence, Abuse, and Conflict in Relationships

- Domestic Violence Information Center <http://www.feminist.org/other/dv/dvhome.html>
  This Web site, from the Feminist Majority Foundation, contains statistics, fact sheets, and hotline resources for every state in the United States.

- Family Problems http://www.personal.psu.edu/faculty/n/x/nxd10/problems.htm#top>
  This Web site contains essays from students at Penn State on issues related to family problems. It includes topics related to death and dying, and alcohol and drug use. These essays are short but provide a good overview of each topic as well as relevant references.

- Family Violence Prevention Fund <http://www.igc.apc.org/fund>
  This resource provides current statistics on incidents of domestic violence in the United States, information for professionals working with victims of domestic violence, and personal stories.

- Intimate Violence <http://www.personal.psu.edu/faculty/n/x/nxd10/violence.htm>
  This Web site contains essays from students at Penn State on issues related to intimate violence including partner and child abuse. These essays are short but provide a good overview of each topic as well as relevant references.

- Men and Women Against Domestic Violence <http://www.silcom.com/~paladin/madv/>
  An Internet-based coalition of men and women working against domestic violence, this Web site contains collected statistics regarding domestic violence, links to related resources on the Web, and domestic violence agencies and hotline numbers by state.

- NOW and Violence Against Women <http://www.now.org/issues/violence/index.html>
  This Web page from the National Organization for Women (NOW), includes a discussion of legal actions, statistics, and current news items related to violence against women. The Web page also may

be accessed from NOW's home page <http://www.now.org>. Select Key Issues and Violence Against Women.

- Sexual Assault Information Page <http://www.cs.utk.edu/~bartley/saInfoPage.html>
  This Web site contains information and links related to sexual assault including acquaintance rape, child sexual abuse, incest, rape, and sexual assault. It also includes information for crisis centers, counseling and support groups, and university resources across the country.

Web Exercise: Resources for Victims of Domestic Violence
Visit the following Web site and learn more about domestic violence: Men and Women Against Domestic Violence <http://www.silcom.com/~paladin/madv/>.

1. What statistics about domestic violence surprised you the most?

2. Where is the nearest organization or shelter to you?

3. What types of services are offered at the nearest organization or shelter? (If this information is not available on the Web, call the organization to find out.)

4. What type of volunteer opportunities are provided there? (If this information is not available on the Web, call the organization to find out.)

5. Write down the phone number in case you or anyone you know needs help or wants to volunteer.

Browse the following Web resources related to domestic violence.
- Family Violence Prevention Fund <http://www.igc.apc.org/fund>
- Sexual Assault Information Page <http://www.cs.utk.edu/~bartley/saInfoPage.html>

INTERNET GLOSSARY

Archie   A search engine for anonymous FTP archives.

ArchiePlex   Web-based interface for using Archie.

bandwidth   The amount of information that can be transferred across a network at one time.

bit   The smallest unit of information in a computer; represented by 0 or 1.

Bookmark   A tool provided by most Web browsers that enables you to save Web page URLs so that you can return to them at any time.

Boolean logic   A system for searching a database that uses the operators AND, OR, and NOT to look for two variables.

bps   A measure of data transmission capacity, used to describe a modem's speed, such as 28.8K bps (or 28,800 bits per second).

browser   An interface for reading information on the World Wide Web, either graphical (such as Navigator or Explorer) or textual (such as Lynx).

bulletin board   (BBS)   Area where users can read and post messages, as well as download files.

byte   A unit of information in a computer, equal to 8 bits.

CD-ROM   (compact disk, read-only memory)   A compact disk used to store and retrieve computer data.

chat   Electronic conversations among Internet users taking place in real time in chat areas (or chat channels, groups, rooms, or sites).

client   The computer and software you use to access Internet servers.

DNS   (domain name system)   The convention for translating the names of hosts into Internet addresses; see also **URL**.

domain name   The part of the Internet address (URL) that specifies the area on a computer reserved for a particular organization, such as mayfieldpub.com. In this example, .com stands for "commercial"; other types of organization designations include .edu for "educational" and .gov for "governmental."

download   To transfer information from one computer to another, or to transfer information from a network to your computer.

e-mail   Electronic mail; one of the most popular uses of the Internet; it can be sent to an individual or a list.

FAQs   (frequently asked questions)   Lists of common questions about a particular product, service, or topic.

file path   Subdirectory in a URL, leading to the specific file you want.

flaming   Sending a large number of angry messages, usually to someone who has broken the rules of netiquette.

freeware   Copyrighted software that is distributed for free and may not be resold.

FTP   (file transfer protocol)   The standard protocol for transferring files across the Internet. Most browsers have one-way FTP; for two-way (the ability to send as well as receive), you can acquire FTP software for both Macintoshes (Fetch) and PCs (WS_FTP).

GIF (graphics interchange format)   File format for images that are viewable on the Web; see also **JPEG.**

Gopher   A menu-driven information system created at the University of Minnesota.

hits   The number of times a particular page is accessed, or the number of successful matches you receive during a key word search.

home page   The main, or starting, page for a series of Web pages.

HTML (hypertext markup language)   The formatting language of the World Wide Web.

HTTP (hypertext transfer protocol)   The protocol for reading HTML programs from the Web.

hyperlink   See **link.**

hypermedia   Links among various kinds of multimedia objects, such as video, audio, and virtual reality, in addition to text and graphics.

hypertext   A text link that takes you to another file on the Internet. A hypertext document contains hypertext or hyperlinks or both.

Internet   A global network of linked computers; home to the World Wide Web, newsgroups, bulletin boards, Gopher, and online forums.

IRC (Internet relay chat)   See **chat**.

ISP (Internet service provider)   A company that provides subscribers access to the Internet.

JPEG or **JPG** (joint photographic expert group)   File format for images that are viewable on the Web; see also **GIF**.

Jughead   A search engine for Gopher document titles.

link   Short for *hyperlink*. A link, textual or graphic, that takes you to another file on the Internet or another location in a document.

listserv   A program that distributes e-mail to a mailing list.

lurk   To browse and read messages, but not actively participate in a discussion group. It's a good idea before joining discussion groups.

mailing list   A discussion group that shares an interest in a particular topic; messages sent by members of the group are e-mailed to all its members.

modem   A device that allows a remote computer to communicate via phone lines to networks and other computers.

MOO (MUD object-oriented environment)   Multi-user environment based on object-oriented programming technology. See **MUD.**

MUD (multi-user domain [dungeon or dimension])   Virtual environment on the Internet primarily used for role-playing games such as Dungeons and Dragons.

MUSH (multi-user shared hallucination)   A MUD variation.

netiquette   Etiquette on the Internet. The guidelines for preferred behavior when communicating with others on the Internet.

network   A system of computers that can transmit information from one to another.

newsgroup   A discussion group, or informal bulletin board, that shares an interest in a particular topic; newsgroups are located on Usenet, where articles are read and posted.

packet   When information is transferred from the Internet to your computer, it is broken into pieces, or packets, which are transmitted to your computer and reassembled by TCP software.

POP (post office protocol)   The standard protocol for reading Internet mail sent using SMTP.

protocol   Information format. The protocol lets two computers know what type of information is being transferred. The protocol for transferring information across the Internet is given in the first part of the URL (e.g., http, ftp, gopher, telnet).

RAM (random access memory)   The amount of available short-term memory in a computer directly correlates to the speed of your processor—the more RAM you have, the faster your computer is.

ROM (read-only memory)   The unchangeable portion of the computer's memory containing the start-up instructions for your system.

search engine   A program that allows you to perform key word searches to locate Web documents.

server   A computer accessible to other networked computers.

shareware   Copyrighted software that is distributed on a trial basis; you eventually have to pay for it if you want to continue to use it beyond the trial period. The cost is generally minimal.

SMTP (simple mail transfer protocol)   The standard protocol for transferring e-mail from one computer to another across the Internet.

spam   Unsolicited e-mail usually sent to a large number of users, such as to a Usenet group or a listserv mailing list.

subject tree   A hierarchical directory of information.

surfing   Aimlessly exploring the Internet by clicking links from one page to another.

tags   Codes used in hypertext markup language (HTML).

TCP/IP (transmission control protocol/Internet protocol)   TCP is the software your computer uses to create an interface with the Internet. TCP software receives the packets of data transmitted across the Internet and reassembles the corresponding file so that you can view the resulting Web page. IP is the protocol that computers use to talk to each other on the Internet, and it helps to define the route packets take.

Telnet   A standard protocol for logging on to another computer remotely. For example, if you want to log on from home to your UNIX account at school, you can use Telnet.

thread   The original newsgroup message (article) and all of its associated replies.

UNIX   A freeware computer operating system used by many colleges and universities.

URL (uniform resource locator)   An address for an Internet location.

Usenet   A UNIX-based computing system used mainly for discussion and newsgroups.

Veronica   A program that searches the full text of Gopher documents.

videoconference   Two or more people interacting through real-time video and audio feeds.

virus   A self-replicating destructive program that can be downloaded from the Internet or obtained via an infected file on a diskette. A few viruses are harmless and even amusing, but most can destroy the data on your hard disk.

Web page   Any Web document viewable with a browser.

World Wide Web   The segment of the Internet that uses primarily HTTP.

WOO (Web object-oriented environment)   A virtual space primarily used for role-playing; similar to MUD, but located on the World Wide Web.

INDEX

FAVORITE WEB SITES

Name of Site: _____

URL: _____

Name of Site: _____

URL: _____

Name of Site: _____

URL: _____

Name of Site: _____

URL: _____

Name of Site: _____

URL: _____

Name of Site: _____

URL: _____

Name of Site: _____

URL: _____

Name of Site: _____

URL: _____

Name of Site: _____

URL: _____

Name of Site: _____

URL: _____

Name of Site: _____

URL: _____

Name of Site: _____

URL: _____

Name of Site: _____

URL: _____

Name of Site: _____

URL: _____

Name of Site: _____

URL: _____

Name of Site: _____

URL: _____

Name of Site: _____

URL: _____

Name of Site: _____

URL: _____

Name of Site: _____

URL: _____

Name of Site: _____

URL: _____

Name of Site: _____

URL: _____

Name of Site: _____

URL: _____

Name of Site: _____

URL: _____

Name of Site: _____

URL: _____

Name of Site: _____

URL: _____

Name of Site: _____

URL: _____

Name of Site: _____

URL: _____

Name of Site: _____

URL: _____

Name of Site: _____

URL: _____

Name of Site: _____

URL: _____

Name of Site: _____

URL: _____

Name of Site: _____

URL: _____

Name of Site: _____

URL: _____

Name of Site: _____

URL: _____

Name of Site: _____

URL: _____

Name of Site: _____

URL: _____

Name of Site: _____

URL: _____

Name of Site: _____

URL: _____

Name of Site: _____

URL: _____

Name of Site: _____

URL: _____

Name of Site: _____

URL: _____

Name of Site: _____

URL: _____